Out Flew the Sabres

THE BATTLE
OF BRANDY STATION
JUNE 9, 1863

by Eric J. Wittenberg and Daniel T. Davis

EMERGING CIVIL WAR SERIES

Chris Mackowski, series editor
Kristopher D. White, chief historian
Daniel T. Davis, emeritus editor

The Emerging Civil War Series:

Out Flew the Sabres

THE BATTLE
OF BRANDY STATION
JUNE 9, 1863

by Eric J. Wittenberg and Daniel T. Davis

EMERGING CIVIL WAR SERIES

SB

Savas Beatie

California

© 2016 by Eric J. Wittenberg and Daniel T. Davis

All rights reserved. No part of this publication may be reproduced, stored in a retrieval system, or transmitted, in any form or by any means, electronic, mechanical, photocopying, recording, or otherwise, without the prior written permission of the publisher. Printed in the United States of America.

First edition, first printing

ISBN-13: 978-1-61121-256-3
eISBN: 978-1-61121-257-0

Library of Congress Control Number: 2015029216

SB

Published by
Savas Beatie LLC
989 Governor Drive, Suite 102
El Dorado Hills, California 95762
Phone: 916-941-6896
Email: sales@savasbeatie.com
Web: www.savasbeatie.com

Savas Beatie titles are available at special discounts for bulk purchases in the United States by corporations, institutions, and other organizations. For more details, please contact Special Sales, P.O. Box 4527, El Dorado Hills, CA 95762, or you may e-mail us as at sales@savasbeatie.com, or visit our website at www.savasbeatie.com for additional information.

DAN: For my dad, Tommy Davis, and my brother, Matt,
who remain my companions to Brandy Station
and other Civil War battlefields

ERIC: For Clark B. "Bud" Hall, without whose
ceaseless efforts to save the Brandy Station battlefield,
it would have been destroyed years ago

Table of Contents

The road near St. James Church (Tour Stop 4) (cm)

List of Maps

Maps by Hal Jespersen

Acknowledgments

We would like to graciously thank Theodore P. Savas and Sarah Keeney of Savas Beatie Publishing and Chris Mackowski, the editor of the Emerging Civil War Series. Once again, they have helped bring a manuscript full circle to fruition. Hal Jespersen worked with us to build a superb set of maps. We thank our colleagues, the wonderful authors at Emerging Civil War—in particular Kris White, who took time away from his schedule to write an excellent foreword that properly framed the battle within the overall context of the Gettysburg campaign. Rob Orrison also contributed some fantastic pictures. Mike Block, vice president of the Friends of the Cedar Mountain Battlefield, contributed an excellent appendix on the Army of the Potomac's 1863-64 Winter Encampment in Culpeper. Jim Lighthizer, president of the Civil War Trust, wrote an afterword detailing the preservation efforts at Brandy Station. Thanks to the monumental efforts of the Trust, future generations will be able to visiting and walking the battlefield.

DAN: I owe a debt of gratitude to Ted and Chris but especially to Eric Wittenberg for bringing me onto this project. Having the opportunity to work with someone of Eric's stature and expertise was both humbling and a wonderful learning experience. My beautiful wife, Katy, continues to be a source of inspiration. To my parents, Tommy and Kathy, along with my brother, Matt, and his wife, Candice, for their continued support. Also to my mother-in-law, Cathy Bowen, and my sister and brother-in-law, Becca and Andy. I also owe a thanks to the rest of my family, friends and battlefield companions: Kristin Simmler, Mike Swartz, and Mia Nam. Lastly, I am especially grateful for my late father-in-law, Tom Bowen. Tom always put others first, whether they were family,

friends, or the people he met on his many mission trips. He is missed by those who love him, but we take comfort knowing he is watching over us still.

Buford's Knoll (Tour Stop 5) (cm)

ERIC: Thank you to Dan Davis for wanting to do this project with me. Dan is a fine historian in his own right, and it was a pleasure to work with him on this book. Thank you to Bud Hall for being the best teacher a student could ever want. I am, as always, endlessly grateful to my wonderful wife, Susan Skilken Wittenberg, without whom none of this could ever occur. Finally, I am grateful to Chris and Ted for their fine work with the Emerging Civil War Series.

PHOTO CREDITS: Mike Block (mb); Daniel T. Davis (dd); Library of Congress (loc); Chris Mackowski (cm); U. S. Army History and Education Center (usahaec); University of South Carolina (usc); Virginia Historical Society (vhs); Williams College (wc); Eric J. Wittenberg (ew)

For the Emerging Civil War Series

Theodore P. Savas, publisher
Chris Mackowski, series editor
Kristopher D. White, chief historian
Sarah Keeney, editorial consultant

Design and layout by Chris Mackowski
with layout assistance from Levi Trimble
Maps by Hal Jespersen

Touring the Battlefield

The battle of Brandy Station and the events related to it cover a wide expanse across Culpeper County. Directions to each stop follow at the end of each chapter.

Eric Wittenberg spends considerable time on the Brandy Station battlefield. (cm)

While much of the driving tour route is along secondary roads, you will have to use major highways such as Route 15/29 and Route 3. Traffic can be heavy along these roads; please exercise caution at all times.

Additionally, there is property along the route that may not be owned by a preservation organization. Please be mindful of all posted signs and respect the owners's rights.

You will also have the opportunity to leave your vehicle and walk the battlefield. The Civil War Trust has installed and maintained trails at stops 3, 4, 5 and 7. Although no trail exists, you may wish to follow the walking directions in chapter 6 to see the stone wall on the Cunningham Farm. Always secure all valuables and lock your vehicle. Additionally, be aware of poison oak and wildlife, especially snakes.

The tour begins—Tour Stop 1—at the Graffiti House, located off Carrico Mills Road.

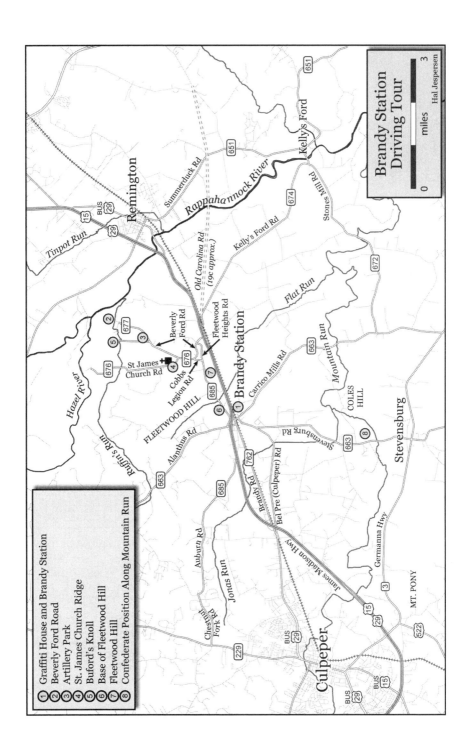

Brandy Station Driving Tour

NO.   13-F

OPENING OF
GETTYSBURG CAMPAIGN

ON THIS PLAIN LEE REVIEWED
HIS CAVALRY, JUNE 8, 1863. THE
NEXT DAY THE CAVALRY BATTLE OF
BRANDY STATION WAS FOUGHT.
ON JUNE 10, EWELL'S CORPS, FROM
ITS CAMP NEAR HERE, BEGAN THE
MARCH TO PENNSYLVANIA.

CONSERVATION AND DEVELOPMENT COMMISSION 1927

Foreword

BY KRISTOPHER D. WHITE

"I have just received information, which I consider reliable," penned Brig. Gen. John Buford, "that all of the available cavalry of the Confederacy is in Culpeper County." More than 9,500 Southern horsemen were massed in the fields around the hamlet of Culpeper, Virginia. Buford, who was arguably the best cavalry officer in the Federal Army of the Potomac, located what would be the vanguard unit of Gen. Robert E. Lee's famed Army of Northern Virginia as it embarked on its summer campaign.

Four days later, Buford's troopers splashed across Beverly's Ford and engaged the enemy in combat, and in the process, touched off the largest cavalry battle of the Civil War.

There is great irony in the fact that the battle of Brandy Station was the first large engagement of what many believe to be the turning point of the American Civil War, the Gettysburg campaign. Although the battle was a Federal defeat, Brandy Station itself stands as a turning point of sorts. It was here that the Federal cavalry finally matured to the point that it could stand toe-to-toe with its Southern counterpart.

*   *   *

A historical marker near Stuart's Review Field, between Brandy Station and Culpeper, foreshadows the coming Gettysburg campaign. (dd)

By the late spring of 1863, a Confederate offensive headed by Lee's army had been a long time coming. Since his defeat at Sharpsburg, Lee had yearned to regain

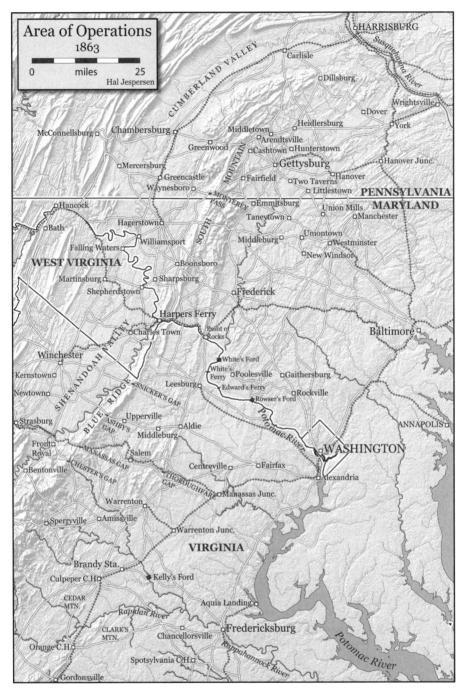

Area of Operations—After Brandy Station, the opposing cavalry continued to spar as the two armies march north from Fredericksburg. The next clash came in the Loudoun Valley in the middle of June. Stuart battled Pleasonton in quick succession at Aldie, Middleburg, and Upperville as the Federals tried to locate Lee's army. The mounted arms met again north of the Mason Dixon line at Hanover, Hunterstown, and Gettysburg.

the initiative that he lost on the banks of Antietam Creek. His dramatic victory at Chancellorsville, in May, 1863, was the catalyst Lee needed for a second campaign across the Potomac. In the days following Chancellorsville, Lee gained the approval from the Confederate high command to keep the momentum and press north towards Maryland and Pennsylvania. Throughout late May, he tirelessly reorganized his army and, by the first week of June, was ready to take the offensive.

Lee's move was a calculated one. Victory at Chancellorsville buoyed Southern hopes of ultimate victory, yet the Southern victory came at a high cost.

More than 13,000 Confederates were casualties as a result of the battle, including Lee's third in command, Thomas J. "Stonewall" Jackson. Lee also lost nine of his 28 brigade commanders and 64 of 130 regimental commanders. By the time the first Southern soldier stepped off towards Pennsylvania, on June 3, more than one-third of all of Lee's infantry brigade commanders were new to their posts, as were two-thirds of his corps commanders.

Despite the heavy attrition in the officer corps, and the reorganization of the army, the time to strike was now. Major General Ulysses S. Grant was threatening the city of Vicksburg, Mississippi. The loss of this key city would give the Union navy unmitigated control of the Mississippi River and cut the Confederacy in two. Even though Vicksburg was 1,000 miles away, Lee was pressured to send troops to relieve that sector. Lee felt that "[t]he distance and the uncertainty of the employment of the troops [transferred there] are unfavorable." In Lee's mind, the best way to ease the pressure on the west "would be for this army to cross into Maryland."

With the hopes of stealing a march on Joe Hooker's Federal army, Lee set his sights on Culpeper, where he had already amassed five cavalry brigades and five batteries of horse artillery. From Culpeper, Lee would aim his army for the gaps in the Blue Ridge Mountains which led to a virtual highway to the Potomac River, the Shenandoah Valley.

* * *

The units of Maj. Gen. Jeb Stuart's famed cavalry

division were made up of veteran officers and men. The mounted arm of Lee's army had been spared the attrition that Lee's infantry commanders endured. While the infantry branch began to lack experience at brigade and regimental level, the void should have been made up for in Lee's mounted arm.

On June 3, 1863, the men of Lee's army broke camp and embarked on a campaign that would take them from the banks of the Rappahannock River in Virginia across the Potomac River and into Pennsylvania. Leaving his newly formed Third Corps along the old Rappahannock line, Lee shifted two-thirds of his infantry to the Culpeper area, where they would link up with the bulk of all of his cavalry. It was the Southern infantry that Jeb Stuart and his cavalry were to screen from the prying eyes of the pesky Union cavalry. Utilizing Culpeper as a staging area, Lee and Stuart amassed more than 50,000 Confederates by the evening of June 8.

The monument to the 1st Massachusetts Cavalry at Aldie is one of the few markers that commemorates the turbulent cavalry actions on the road to Gettysburg. (dd)

The next day, June 9, Stuart was to set off north across Welford's and Beverly's fords as the screening force for Lee's Second Corps and the rest of the army. The god of war is fickle, and rather than being at the forefront of a march, Stuart's men were locked in mortal combat at Brandy Station. Through skill, audacity, and a great deal of luck, Stuart held his own in the battle. Southern troopers prevented the Federals from viewing Lee's massing army; maintaining the secrecy that Lee so greatly desired.

"Comrades! two [sic] divisions of the enemy's cavalry and artillery, escorted by a strong force of infantry, tested your mettle and found it proof-steel," Stuart wrote proudly to his men after their hard won victory, "Your saber blows, inflicted on that glorious day, have taught them again the weight of Southern vengeance . . . . An act of rashness on his part was severely punished by rout and loss of his artillery. With an abiding faith in the God of battles, and a firm reliance on the saber, your successes will continue."

While Stuart should have been proud of the way his men performed, his own performance was mixed at best—for the second time in three months, the Federals got the jump on the vaunted Southern cavalier. Rather than leading and screening the Army of Northern Virginia north, Stuart's men were forced to stay in the Culpeper area until June 15 just in case the Federals reared their ugly heads again. In the meantime, Lt. Gen. Richard S. Ewell's 22,000 men started for Chester Gap in the Blue Ridge. By June 12, Ewell's men were in Port Royal, and on the 13th, Confederate's were closing in on Union garrisons at Berryville, and Winchester.

For the first few days Ewell's men lacked cavalry support on the march, but were met by Brig. Gen. Albert Jenkins's 1,800 troopers. Jenkins's men were new addition to Lee's army and had not been not present at Brandy Station.

On June 15, sensing that the Federal threat in the Culpeper area had passed, Lee released Stuart for his primary mission: screening the march north. The same day Stuart's troopers set off toward the Potomac, Ewell's men were crossing it.

The Confederate army was teeming with luck as it set off on the campaign. Joe Hooker's initial lethargic reactions to Lee's maneuvers, coupled with his lackluster cavalry commander, enabled the Confederates to slip away from Hooker's army with relative ease. Although Hooker forced a crossing below Fredericksburg on June 5, the Federals did not press their luck. Had they, they could have stopped Lee's offensive in its infant stages while also threatening the destruction of the Confederate Third Corps.

Hooker's cavalry commander, Brig. Gen. Alfred Pleasonton, failed in his mission on June 9 to "disperse and destroy" Stuart's cavalry. Pleasonton also failed to accurately locate nearly two-thirds of the Confederate

"WE TRIED TO DO OUR DUTY LIKE BRAVE MEN."

—*Judson Kilpatrick*

infantry amasses in the Culpeper area. In the days following Brandy Station, Hooker and Pleasonton were under the impression that they had "prevent[ed] Stuart from making his raid, which he was to have commenced this morning [June 10]." While Pleasonton did prevent Stuart from commencing a movement, it was not a raid—rather, it was the Lee's second invasion of the north, and Brandy Station had been the first major engagement of a new campaign.

Although Lee was "marching on," the Union cavalry held a new confidence. "For the first time we have fought as a brigade. We tried to do our duty like brave men. I am proud of my brigade," touted soon-to-be Brig. Gen. Judson Kilpatrick. Brandy Station was that turning point the Army of the Potomac's cavalry needed. They had proven they could stand toe-to-toe with the best Stuart could throw at them. While there were still a few command issues to work out, Hooker's mounted corps was finally working as a well-oiled machine.

Over the next few weeks, the Federal cavalry rode hard and fought hard against a foe that was starting to give them grudging respect. Hooker's army began lurching forward as he finally realized the enemy was pressing north. On June 17, the Federal cavalry fought desperately at Aldie, while Stuart protected James Longstreet's First Corps as they made their way into the Shenandoah Valley. Two days later, the Federals tried their hand against Stuart again to no avail. On June 21, another desperate engagement brought the two cavalry forces together at Upperville. The Federals again came close to besting Stuart, but pulling back to Ashby's Gap again blocked the Federal access to the valley.

Stuart had managed to thwart Pleasonton's troopers at every turn—but then Stuart's Achille's heel came into play. Stuart sought permission to make a ride around Hooker's army. Lee consented. Taking three brigades with him, Stuart set-off on his now infamous ride. Badly miscalculating the speed and disposition of the Federals, Stuart was forced time and again to extend his route, essentially taking himself out of the campaign from June 24-July 2. Although Stuart left Lee with four brigades of cavalry to utilize during the campaign, Lee

KRISTOPHER D. WHITE, *a former Licensed Battlefield Guide at Gettysburg and NPS historian, is the chief historian and co-founder of Emerging Civil War.*

employed them poorly, and Stuart, who was Lee's best reconnaissance officer, essentially blinded the Southern army when they needed him the most.

During the time Stuart took himself off the table, the Federals proved their mettle. On the morning of June 30, Jeb Stuart bit off more than he could chew at the battle of Hanover. While trying to locate the main Confederate body, Stuart was nearly captured as he tangled with aggressive Federal cavalry. Meanwhile, later in the afternoon, Yankee troopers located the main Confederate army west of the town of Gettysburg. The next morning, the Federals fought a magnificent delaying action that bought enough time to bring the Army of the Potomac onto the field. On July 2, at Hunterstown, a soon-to-be-famous George Custer cut his teeth at brigade-level command, and David Gregg helped to secure the Union right flank by holding the famed Stonewall Brigade at bay along Brinkerhoff's Ridge. Those same troopers helped bring home that long-awaited decisive victory over Lee's men at Gettysburg and Stuart's men on East Cavalry Field.

Yet, of the 103 actions, skirmishes, engagements, and battles in the Gettysburg campaign, Brandy Station represents the first turning in the war's most famous action. It was not a turning point that shifted the course of the entire war; it was the turning point in the confidence of the men who took to the saddle for the Army of the Potomac. One of Stuart's staff officers lamented after the war, "One result of incalculable importance certainly did follow this battle,—it made the Federal cavalry. Up to that time confessedly inferior to the Southern horsemen, they gained on this day that confidence in themselves and in their commanders which enabled them to contest so fiercely the subsequent battle-fields of June, July, and October."

That ferocity and confidence that the Federals showed at Brandy Station blossomed into victory as they fought the campaign at McPherson Ridge, Brinkerhoff Ridge, and East Cavalry Field. The victories on those fields to come were foreshadowed by the fighting on Fleetwood Hill, at Beverly Ford, and around St. James Church.

The Michigan Brigade, consisting of the 1st, 5th, 6th, and 7th Regiments, played a crucial role in the Union victory on East Cavalry Field at Gettysburg. The monument dedication, which took place on June 18, 1889, was attended by Michigan's governor. (dd)

"Out flew the sabres,
and most handsomely they were used."

— *Brig. Gen. John Buford*

Prologue

Twenty-six-year-old Maj. Robert Morris, Jr. patiently sat on his horse, waiting for instructions that warm spring morning. The major, the namesake of his great-grandfather, Robert Morris, the financier of the American Revolution, commanded the 6th Pennsylvania Cavalry, a veteran regiment made up of mostly Philadelphians. Only five companies of the 6th Pennsylvania Cavalry were present with him on that day; the others were off doing detached duty elsewhere. He heard carbine fire popping in their front as the troopers of Col. Benjamin F. "Grimes" Davis's cavalry brigade skirmished with grayclad horsemen in their front. Not knowing that Davis was dead and that his brigade had become demoralized as a result, Major Morris and his men crossed the Rappahannock River at Beverly's Ford with the rest of the Reserve Brigade. They then filed up Beverly's Ford Road until they came to a thick stand of woods half a mile or so away from the main line of Confederate cavalry. They halted there, awaiting further orders as they listened to the incessant popping of carbines nearby.

Morris did not have long to wait.

Before long, an orderly reined in. "General Buford sends his compliments and directs you to clear those woods in front of you," he declared. Morris heard the instructions, nodded, and turned to address his troopers. He formed up his five companies into a line of battle. They then moved out at a slow walk, trying to maintain their formation in the thick woods, which

The road along the St. James Church ridge provided Federals with a straight landmark to guide on during their attack—but it provided Confederates with the perfect spot to mount an ambush, too. (cm)

was no small task. Nearing the edge of the woods, Morris barked out, "Draw!" and then 'Sabers!" A metallic clang rang out up and down the line as the Pennsylvanians drew their sabers from their scabbards.

Cavalry of Brig. Gen. William E. "Grumble" Jones' brigade, deployed in a field in front of the Confederate main line of battle, heard the distinctive sound of the sabers being drawn and watched as the line of Pennsylvanians came out of the tree line. Realizing that they were about to receive a cavalry charge, they began preparing. The long line of Southern artillery on the distant ridgeline began belching death at the proud Pennsylvania horsemen, who struggled to maintain their formation as if they were still on a parade ground.

The intensity of the Southern carbine fire increased as the Federal horse soldiers continued their steady advance. "Forward! Guide right! March!" barked out Major Morris. About 20 paces later, he cried, "Trot, march!" Clumps of sod began flying from underneath of the hooves of the horses as they accelerated to a trot. About 60 paces farther on, the major sang out, "Gallop, march!" as the regiment's buglers echoed the command over the din of battle, which grew louder with each step.

Blasts of canister from the Confederate artillery began bursting among the charging Pennsylvanians, who remained determined to reach their objective: the long line of guns blasting away at them. Quickly closing on the guns, Major Morris pointed his saber and screamed, "CHARGE!" The Union bugles sounded the call for the charge, and his men put spurs to their horses, pointed their sabers as the major had, and dashed toward the guns, which drew nearer with each step of their panting horses. A determined Union cheer rang out as the horsemen rapidly closed on the line of guns, which was now only a few yards away.

The sight of this brave, determined charge briefly transfixed the Southern artillerists and cavalrymen as they admired the discipline and good order of Morris' command. They quickly shook off their reverie and prepared to receive the tidal wave that was about to crash over them. Samuel L. Gracey, the chaplain of the 6th Pennsylvania Cavalry, who

Taken in 1860, this image depicts Robert Morris, second from left, as a First Sergeant in the First City Troop, Philadelphia City Cavalry. Morris was the great-grandson of the financier of the American Revolution, Robert Morris. A militia unit, the Philadelphia City Cavalry was organized in 1774 and served as George Washington's personal bodyguard. Recruited from Philadelphia's upper society, membership was by election only, and the troopers did not accept pay for their service. Many of its officers served in the 6th Pennsylvania Cavalry. (ew)

witnessed the magnificent scene unfolding in front of him, wrote admiringly, "The Philadelphia men rode hard across the open field toward their date with destiny, their company guidons snapping in the warm spring breeze."

It was June 9, 1863, and this was the battle of Brandy Station, the largest cavalry battle ever fought on the North American continent. And for the cavalrymen of both sides, nothing would ever be the same when it was over.

"THE PHILADELPHIA MEN RODE HARD ACROSS THE OPEN FIELD TOWARD THEIR DATE WITH DESTINY, THEIR COMPANY GUIDONS SNAPPING IN THE WARM SPRING BREEZE."

— *Chaplain of the 6th PA Cavalry*

The Confederate Cavalry Concentrates

CHAPTER ONE

In the first week of May 1863, Gen. Robert E. Lee and the Confederate Army of Northern Virginia defeated Maj. Gen. Joseph Hooker's Union Army of the Potomac at the battle of Chancellorsville. It was Lee's second decisive defeat of the Federals in five months. Emboldened by his success and determined to retain the initiative, Lee decided to carry the war out of Virginia and invade the North.

With the blessing of the Confederate government, Lee began pulling out of his positions around Fredericksburg in early June. The first Confederate troops to leave belonged to Lt. Gen. Richard S. Ewell's Second Corps, who departed on June 4. After a leisurely march, Ewell's infantry arrived in and around Culpeper Court House, west of Fredericksburg, three days later. Waiting for them were Maj. Gen. James Ewell Brown Stuart's cavalry division.

J. E. B. Stuart, Lee's cavalry chief, had arrived in Culpeper on May 20 and established his headquarters to oversee the concentration of the Confederate horses in preparation for the coming invasion. Within a few days of Stuart's arrival, three brigades of Southern horse soldiers also arrived, establishing their camps in the lush fields of Culpeper County. On May 22, Stuart reviewed about 4,500 of his command, comprising the brigades of Brig. Gens. Wade Hampton, Fitzhugh Lee, and W. H. F. "Rooney" Lee. A Confederate staff officer remembered, "The grand Cavalry Review took place this morning and was one of the most imposing

A monument to Confederate artillerist John Pelham stands today near the Graffiti House. Pelham was a rising star in the Army of Northern Virginia when he was killed in March 1863 at the nearby battle of Kelly's Ford. The monument was erected in 1926 by George and Lenora Douglas with support from the Pelham Chapter of the United Daughters of the Confederacy (Birmingham, AL). Originally placed at an out-of-the way location, the monument was moved to its current location in May 2013. (cm)

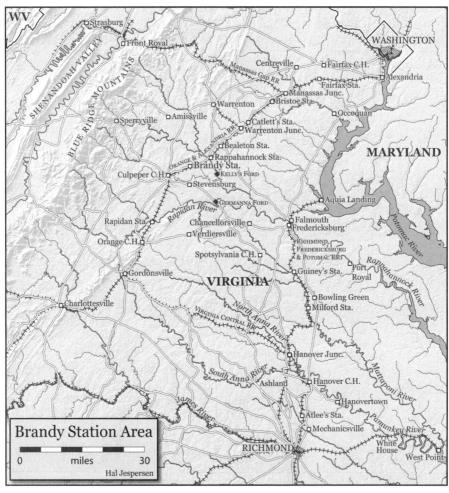

BRANDY STATION AREA—In an effort to maintain the momentum gained at his victories at Fredericksburg and Chancellorsville, Gen. Robert E. Lee decided to once again invade the North. In early June 1863, he began to move his Army of Northern Virginia away from their lines at Fredericksburg toward the Shenandoah Valley. To support the movement, Lee ordered his cavalry, under Maj. Gen. J.E.B. Stuart, to concentrate in Culpeper County. Stuart chose Brandy Station as his encampment because the area offered open farmland and plenty of forage for his horses. Stuart's presence, however, did not go unnoticed by the Union cavalry, which determined to spoil his respite prior to the opening of the summer campaign.

scenes I ever witnessed." The following evening, Stuart threw a magnificent cotillion in Culpeper attended by his officers and the local ladies.

Meanwhile, Hooker fretted over Stuart and his motives. Unnerved by the massing of the Confederate cavalry and probably hoping to regain some pride after his recent drubbing, he resolved to "send all my

After a stinging loss at the hands of Robert E. Lee at Chancellorsville, Joseph Hooker tried to lay new plans. Before he could execute any of them, he first had to disrupt the concentration of enemy cavalry beyond his far right flank. (loc)

cavalry against" the assembling mass of Confederate horsemen, in an attempt "to break . . . up [the offensive] in its incipiency." Accordingly, Brig. Gen. Alfred Pleasonton, the temporary commander of the Army of the Potomac's Cavalry Corps, ordered Brig. Gen. John Buford, commanding the First Cavalry Division, to march to Bealeton. There, Buford would join Brig. Gen. David M. Gregg's Second Cavalry Division and reconnoiter the upper Rappahannock in an effort to discern Stuart's intentions.

Buford's and Gregg's efforts detected the presence of a very large force of enemy cavalry encamped in the vicinity of Culpeper Courthouse. After forwarding this information to army headquarters, Hooker correctly surmised that the Confederates were concentrating to screen a major advance down the Shenandoah Valley. Hooker ordered Buford to spare no effort to ascertain the objective of the Confederate movement and declared that "at all events, they have no business on this side of the [Rappahannock]."

Still, the Federals encountered difficulties. They were unable to locate Stuart's exact position, which did little to assuage Hooker's anxiety.

Then on June 5, Buford's determined scouting paid off. "I have just received information, which I consider reliable, that all of the available cavalry of the Confederacy is in Culpeper County," he wrote. The Kentuckian informed headquarters that the brigades of Brig. Gen. Fitzhugh Lee, Brig. Gen. William H. F. Lee, Brig. Gen. Beverly Robertson, Brig. Gen. Albert

Basking in the successes at Fredericksburg and Chancellorsville, for the second time in nine months Confederate commander Robert E. Lee decided on a second invasion of the North. (loc)

LEFT: New to command of the Cavalry Corps in the Army of the Potomac, the ambitious Alfred Pleasonton hoped to enhance his reputation by engaging the Confederates in open battle. (loc)

RIGHT: A Kentuckian by birth, John Buford remained in the U.S. Army when Southern states started to secede. Buford commanded a brigade of cavalry during the Second Manassas Campaign and proved to be an excellent horse soldier. His intelligence gathering in the weeks following the battle of Chancellorsville were essential in the development of the Union plan of attack. (loc)

G. Jenkins, and Brig. Gen. William E. Jones had all arrived in Culpeper. For the most part, Buford's report was accurate, although Jenkins' men were not present.

At the same time, the Federal cavalry grew restless. The blue troopers spent their days drilling, racing their horses, and listening to the rumbling of distant artillery. Soon, there would be more drastic tasks at hand to occupy their time.

The same day that Buford submitted his report, Pleasonton notified Hooker that Stuart's pickets extended all the way to the Blue Ridge Mountains, which further indicated preparations for a massive Confederate movement. Determined to disrupt the Rebel plans, Pleasonton instructed Buford to "make a strong demonstration without delay upon the enemy in your front toward Culpeper." Buford obeyed and immediately engaged the enemy in skirmishing that was intended to determine the size of the Confederate force in his front.

Two days later, after collating all available reports, Hooker's chief of military intelligence, Col. George H. Sharpe, reported his conclusions to the army commander. Sharpe stated that the Confederates intended to launch a massive cavalry raid, "the most important expedition ever attempted in this country." He estimated the size of Stuart's force at 12-15,000 troopers, and believed the gray infantry were preparing to move south to Richmond before moving to reinforce Confederate armies in the west. Although Sharpe misread Stuart's specific objective, he correctly divined that a major expedition was in the offing.

Taking these reports into account, Hooker decided to proceed with caution. Buford's diligent troopers continued sending back word of their findings. The day before Sharpe's report, Buford informed headquarters, "Yesterday cannon firing was heard toward Culpeper. I suppose it was a salute, as I was told Stuart was to have had that day an inspection of his whole force." To reinforce his previous findings, Buford reported, "there is a very heavy cavalry force on the grazing grounds in Culpeper County."

The division commander convinced Hooker that Sharpe's estimates were correct. Hooker wired President Abraham Lincoln, indicating his "great desire to 'bust [Stuart's contemplated raid] up' before it got fairly under way." Joe Hooker began planning an expedition to spoil Stuart's plans.

At Graffiti House and Brandy Station

Remnants from soldiers in blue and gray—sketched in pencil—still adorn the walls of the Graffiti House. (cm)(cm)

Built in 1858 by local resident John Stone, the headquarters of the Brandy Station Foundation derives its name from the amount of graffiti left behind by Union and Confederate soldiers. Inside, you may view it along with exhibits about the battle. The house is open from 11 a.m. to 4 p.m. Friday through Sunday year round, and on Federal holidays that occur on a Monday. The house played no role in the battle.

Brandy Station was an otherwise obscure stop on the Orange & Alexandria Railroad, situated six miles north of Culpeper, best known as a weighing and shipping point for lumber, cattle, grain, and ore. Before it became a village, a deep well made it an important stopping point for travelers. A tavern located there known as the Brandy House was renowned for the quality of its brandy during the War of 1812, prompting soldiers to write the word "brandy" on the tavern walls. The owner then wrote the word "Brandy" on a nearby board fence, and when the railroad was constructed in 1852, the word "Station" was added to the sign, giving the place its unusual name. Before long, that name became synonymous with cavalry

fighting during the Civil War—there were four separate large-scale cavalry battles at Brandy Station over the course of the conflict.

This wartime sketch of Brandy Station depicts the buildings around the railroad stop. (loc)

Surrounded by rolling fields and woods, the hamlet's road network played a critical part in the coming battle. One of the main thoroughfares was the Beverly Ford Road. Crossing the Rappahannock, it ran for two miles to another ridgeline occupied by St. James Church. Continuing south, the road skirted the eastern face of a long north-south ridge called Fleetwood Hill, which dominates the landscape.

Across the street from the Graffiti House is a monument to Lt. Col. John Pelham (his promotion from major came posthumously). Interestingly, the monument is not related to the battle of Brandy Station at all. Hailing from Alabama, Pelham left West Point just prior to graduation in the spring of 1861 when his state seceded. A veteran of First Manassas, Pelham distinguished himself as the commander of Stuart's Horse Artillery at Antietam and Fredericksburg, earning him the nickname "the Gallant Pelham." Rising to the rank of lieutenant colonel, he was mortally wounded at the battle of Kelly's Ford on March 17, 1863. He died in Culpeper that night. Erected in 1926 by the United Daughters of the Confederacy, the monument was originally located at the intersection of James Madison Highway (Route 15/29) and Beverly Ford Road (Route 676).

GPS: 38° 30.167′N, 77° 53.411′W

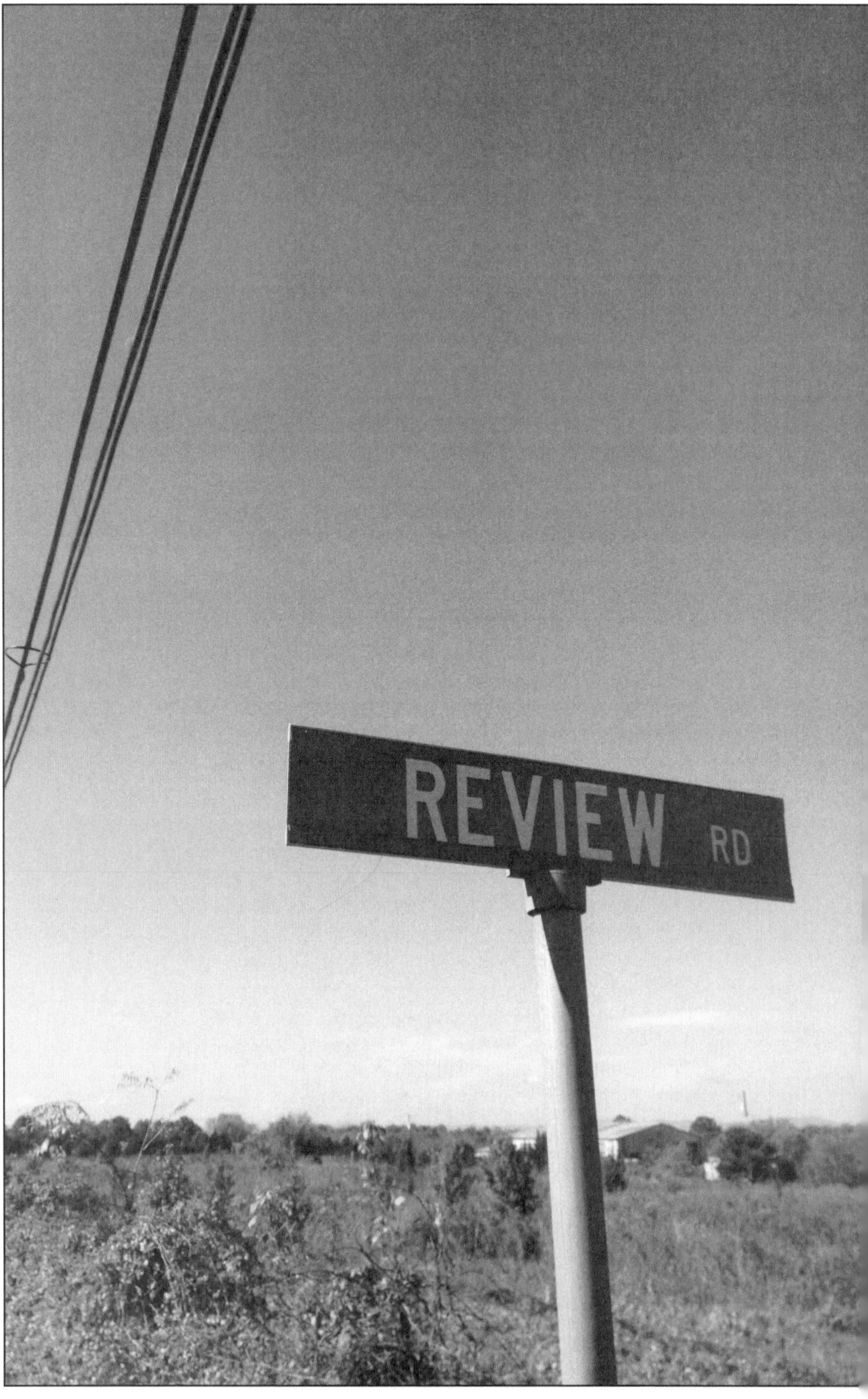
REVIEW RD

Stuart's Grand Reviews

CHAPTER TWO

While Buford and the Federals scouted, analyzed intelligence, and prepared for a foray across the Rappahannock, J. E. B. Stuart engaged in other activities. Now that his cavalry had consolidated, Stuart wanted to show off its strength and planned to hold a review of his division prior to the general movement north. He had held a review of his troopers already on May 22 but planned for a much more magnificent display for the coming days. An officer from the 12th Virginia Cavalry wrote that the spectacle was to "be an imposing sight." Part of the review would include "a sham fight and charge artillery loaded with blank cartridges." Anticipating its pageantry, the dashing Stuart held a "Sabers and Roses Ball" at Culpeper Court House on the evening of June 4.

The following day, local ladies along with Southern dignitaries turned out to watch Stuart and his vaunted cavaliers. In attendance were Sen. Louis T. Wigfall of Texas, former Secretary of War George Randolph, and the current Secretary of War James A. Seddon.

"The effect was thrilling," an officer remembered as the columns passed in review. Stuart appeared "young, gay, and handsome, dressed out in his newest uniform, his polished sword . . . the personification of grace and gallantry combined." The excitement of the day was amplified when he announced that another review would take place three days later and under the critical eye of Robert E. Lee.

While the length of the Review Field can still be traversed, much of the area has been overtaken by modern development. (cm)

Known for his flamboyant appearance, Maj. Gen. J. E. B. Stuart was one of the finest intelligence officers North or South. His ride around the Army of the Potomac prior to the Seven Days' battles and his raiding during the Second Manassas Campaign had provided invaluable information to Robert E. Lee. (loc)

On June 8, Lee and his subordinates, Lt. Gens. James Longstreet and Richard S. Ewell, along with several other generals, turned out to see the cavalry. Brigadier General Fitzhugh Lee, one of Stuart's brigade commanders, invited his old friend Maj. Gen. John Bell Hood, who headed one of Longstreet's divisions, "to bring any of his friends." Announcing that they were "all his friends," Hood appeared with his entire division. "[T]heir presence only increased the ambition of the troopers to do their best," one of the horse artillerists recalled.

Unlike the review a few days earlier, "this was a business affair." A Tar Heel trooper wrote, "marshaled on the plain were one hundred and five squadrons of cavalry, six light field batteries, ambulances with their trained corps of field attendants, etc." Stuart's engineer, Capt. William W. Blackford, fondly remembered that Stuart's command was "at its zenith of power and efficiency."

The Confederate horsemen assembled at Auburn, a farm owned by John Minor Botts. Their lines stretched for some three miles. A captain from the 6th Virginia recalled that "Stuart's eyes gleamed with peculiar brightness as he glanced along this line of cavalry in battle array."

From a low knoll near the Orange & Alexandria Railroad, Lee looked on approvingly. For William L. Wilson of the 12th Virginia, it was the first time he had ever seen Lee. "Even his personal appearance indicates great mental endowment and nobility of soul," he testified.

With Stuart at his side, Lee rode "some six miles at full run for our horses . . . down the line and up again" inspecting the troopers. Lee resumed his old position and, said a witness,

> at the sound of the bugle, taken up and repeated along the line, the corps of horsemen broke by right wheel into columns of squadron, and moving south for a short distance, the head of the column was turned to the left, and again to the left, moving in this new direction, whence it passed immediately in front of the commanding general. It was a splendid military pageant, and an inspiring

LEFT: Brig. Gen. Wade Hampton had been a successful planter prior to the war and entered the Confederate service with no formal military training. Wounded at First Manassas, Hampton returned and proved to be a capable officer. (loc)

RIGHT: A West Point graduate, Brig. Gen. Fitzhugh Lee had steadily risen through the Confederate ranks since the beginning of the war to become one of Stuart's favorite subordinates. (usahec)

scene . . . as this long line of horsemen, in columns of squadron, with nearly ten thousand sabers flashing in the sun light . . . passed in review before the greatest soldier of modern times.

The review lasted for several hours. "This was the last of our frolics for a long time," Captain Blackford lamented "for on the morrow we were to begin the fighting which was kept up almost daily until two weeks after the Battle of Gettysburg."

Lee was impressed. The next day he wrote to his wife, "It was a splendid sight. The men and horses looked well."

Presenting a stark contrast were Lee's relatives serving under Stuart. Lee's son, the 6'3" Brig. Gen. William H. F. "Rooney" Lee, rode Fancy, his massive black charger, while the general's nephew, Fitz, was relegated to sitting on the ground, sidelined by rheumatism. Colonel Thomas T. Munford of the 2nd Virginia Cavalry commanded Fitz's brigade during his absence.

Despite the grand show of military might, Brig. Gen. William "Grumble" Jones bedded down that night with a sense of uneasiness. His men went on picket duty with "our saddled and bridled horses . . . our boots on, and sabers and pistols buckled around us and our carbines at our sides."

"No doubt," Jones prophetically stated, "the Yankees, who have two divisions of cavalry on the other side of the river . . . will want to know what is going on and if I am not mistaken will be over early in the morning to investigate."

Along the Review Field

Proceed straight out of the parking lot of the Graffiti House along Business Route 15/29 (Brandy Road) and continue on for 0.9 miles to the bridge over Jonas Run. This is the southern end of the review field. Stuart held reviews of his cavalry in the area to your right. Major Henry B. McClellan, Stuart's adjutant, recalled that on June 8, "Eight thousand cavalry passed under the eye of their commander, in column of squadrons, first at a walk, and then at the charge, while the guns of the artillery battalion, on the hill opposite the stand, gave forth fire and smoke,

The open fields between Brandy Station (above) and Culpeper provided ample room for Stuart's showmanship. Today, the railroad still runs parallel to those fields, many of which remain open. (loc)

and seemed almost to convert the pageant into real warfare. It was a brilliant day, and the thirst for the 'pomp and circumstance' of war was fully satisfied."

Proceed 1.5 miles until you near the exit for James Madison Highway (Route 15/29). In the open clearing to your right is where the review stand was located. It was here that Lee watched the cavalry pass before him. A cavalryman wrote that the column marched

> until it came within some fifty or one hundred paces of the position occupied by the reviewing general, when squadron by squadron would take up first the trot, then the gallop, until they had passed some distance beyond, when again they would pull down to the walk. After passing in review, the several brigades were brought again to the position which they occupied in the line, whence they were dismissed, one by one, to their respective camps.

Turn right onto Route 15/29 North. After you merge onto the highway, after 0.9 miles, the white house in the field to your left front and across the highway is Auburn, the home of John Minor Botts, who owned the property where the reviews were held. A Unionist and former U.S. Congressman, Botts purportedly acquired the farm through nefarious means from John G. Beckham, whose son, Robert, served as Stuart's chief of artillery and was the unsung hero of the battle.

Throughout the course of June 9, Gen. Robert E. Lee waited anxiously for word of the outcome of the fighting in Culpeper. As the battle intensified, Lee himself rode forward to the Beauregard House, which you will see in Chapter 8, to watch the fighting. While Lee was unwilling to commit infantry troops to support Stuart and potentially allowing the enemy to learn of the proximity of his infantry, Lee ordered Confederate Maj. Gen. Robert Rodes' Second Corps division to advance to Auburn. Two brigades of Rodes' division under Brig. Gen. Junius Daniel and Col. Edward A. O'Neal took up a position on Botts' estate. Fortunately for Lee, they were never forced to enter the battle.

Looking south toward the Review Field from John Botts's property around Auburn. This was one of Stuart's campsites prior to the battle. (dd)

➡ TO STOP 2

Proceed on Route 15/29 past Auburn. In 2.4 miles, through the stoplight at the intersection of Route 15/29 and Alanthus Road, look to your left. This imminence is Fleetwood Hill. "Fleetwood Heights," a Virginia cavalryman recalled, "is a beautiful location that commands the country and roads . . . [at] Brandy Station."

Continue 1.4 miles to the next stoplight. Turn left at this light onto Beverly Ford Road (Route 676). In 1.8 miles the road will turn to gravel. Continue on for another mile until you reach the turn about. Pull around so that you are facing the opposite direction.

GPS: 38° 54.412′ N, 77° 84.881′ W

The Union Plan of Attack

CHAPTER THREE

Brigadier General Alfred Pleasonton was fully aware that there was a strong force of Confederate cavalry on the south bank of the Rappahannock. What he did not know, however, was the exact location of Stuart's encampment. Even more troubling for the upcoming operation was the possibility of encountering Lee's infantry. If Stuart could call on infantry for help, he would have a decided edge in the upcoming fight. To help even the odds, Pleasonton requested that Hooker send infantry support to augment his cavalry.

In turn, Hooker dispatched two brigades under Brig. Gens. David A. Russell and Adelbert Ames. Their command consisted of some of the finest regiments the Army of the Potomac could offer. Russell and Ames each would take with them 1,500 men who would join the cavalry. A soldier from the 3rd Wisconsin in Ames' demi-brigade remembered, "The command was to be . . . well-disciplined . . . capable of marching rapidly and with endurance, with officers noted for energy and efficiency."

Hooker wrote to his cavalry chief: "From the most reliable information at these headquarters, it is recommended that you cross the Rappahannock at Beverley and Kelly's Fords, and march directly on Culpeper." Then, Pleasonton was to split his force and move to "disperse and destroy the Rebel force assembled in the vicinity of Culpeper, and to destroy his trains and supplies of all description to the utmost of your ability." Pleasonton was instructed to "keep

Federal cavalry would attack along the Beverly Ford Road early in the morning; later in the day, they would withdraw along the same route. (cm)

Adelbert Ames was a prime pick to lead the Federal infantry support. His actions at First Manassas would later earn him the Medal of Honor. (loc)

your infantry force together . . . to rally on at all times, which no cavalry force can be able to shake." Should Pleasonton be successful in driving Stuart from the field, he was to aggressively follow the Rebels and destroy them. His orders in hand, Pleasonton made his final preparations.

The same day that Lee reviewed Stuart's cavalry on Botts's farm, Col. Alfred Duffié moved his Second Cavalry Division to Kelly's Ford. There, he was to join Brig. Gen. David Gregg's Third Cavalry Division for the push across the river. A trooper of the 1st Pennsylvania remembered the arduous march from Warrenton: "Slowly pursuing our way through the heat and clouds of dust . . . over parched and arid fields, we at length reached the vicinity of the river, and at nine p.m., bivouacked for the night." They were about a mile from Kelly's Ford.

The next morning, Pleasonton's combined force of 9,000 cavalrymen and 3,000 infantrymen would give battle to Stuart and his vaunted horsemen.

*   *   *

Pleasonton placed Brig. Gen. John Buford in command of the right wing of the operation. This wing included Buford's own First Division and Ames's brigade of selected infantry regiments. Augmenting Buford were several batteries of Federal horse artillery, which added firepower to an already formidable force. Gregg would command the left wing, consisting of his Third Division, Duffié's Second Division, and Russell's infantry.

Adhering to Hooker's orders, Buford was to cross the Rappahannock at Beverly Ford, proceed to Brandy Station and await Gregg's Second Division. Gregg, along with Duffié, would cross six miles downriver at Kelly's Ford. While Gregg met Buford, Duffié would ride to Stevensburg and secure Gregg's left flank. Believing that Stuart was in Culpeper, Buford and Gregg would then push on to that place and engage the Confederates. Should enemy infantry be present, Ames and Russell would be brought up to support the cavalry. The Yankee troopers packed three days' rations for pursuing their routed foe.

Pleasonton's plan was well thought out. But unbeknownst to him, it was based on faulty intelligence. Rather than being encamped around Culpeper, Stuart posted Grumble Jones' brigade and all of his horse artillery on the south bank opposite Beverly Ford. They stood directly in Buford's path. Beverly Robertson's troopers blocked Gregg's route of advance at Kelly's Ford. Stuart had positioned Fitz Lee's brigade, under Tom Munford at Stark's Ford, while Rooney Lee's brigade guarded Welford's Ford. Wade Hampton camped in the countryside between Brandy Station and Stevensburg.

With his troopers covering the crossings within easy supporting distance of one another and reserves close at hand, it would be relatively easy for Stuart to concentrate against either wing. These dispositions would also make it very difficult for Buford and Gregg to concentrate, let alone cooperate in concert.

Unbeknownst to them, Pleasonton's troopers were riding into the teeth of Stuart's command. The battle would not only have a lasting effect on them but the infant campaign as well.

Augustus Ellis was not a professional soldier. He had been an attorney in New York and a fireman in California before the war. Although he'd survive Brandy Station, Ellis would have less than a month to live after the battle: he would be killed leading his regiment at Gettysburg. (loc)

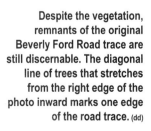

At Beverly Ford

To your left and on the other side of the barbedwire fence are the remains of the Beverly Ford Road, which led through the woods beyond to Beverly Ford on the Rappahannock. Both the trace and ford are on private property, so please respect the owners' rights. Remain at this stop for the next chapter.

Despite the vegetation, remnants of the original Beverly Ford Road trace are still discernable. The diagonal line of trees that stretches from the right edge of the photo inward marks one edge of the road trace. (dd)

The Battle Begins

CHAPTER FOUR

By midnight on June 8, the wings of Pleasonton's command had reached their jumping-off points along the north bank of the Rappahannock. The chaplain of the 6th Pennsylvania Cavalry wrote that no fires were allowed and supper was "cold ham and hard tack." The Pennsylvanians, he remembered, "spread our saddle-blankets on the ground, and with saddles for pillows, prepare for a night's rest. Our minds are full of the coming battle on the morrow, and various speculations are indulged in regard to our prospects of success."

While high ground along the river shielded the troopers from enemy pickets, the men had plenty of time to contemplate what would happen in the morning. One trooper remembered "the morrow will soon break upon us, full of danger and death."

Around two o'clock on the morning of June 9, Buford's troopers stirred. Mounting up, they quietly made their way through dense fog toward Beverly Ford, arriving at their destination two and a half hours later. The depth of the river there was three and a half feet deep. Buford passed instructions to Col. Benjamin F. "Grimes" Davis, commanding his First Brigade, to cross the river and advance in a column of fours and clear out any Confederate pickets on his front.

Under the eye of Pleasonton, Davis led his men into the river, with each successive company receiving the order to draw sabers as they crossed. The first to cross was Davis' old regiment, the 8th New York, which was

Artillery Park field today belies the calm that once crashed through. (cm)

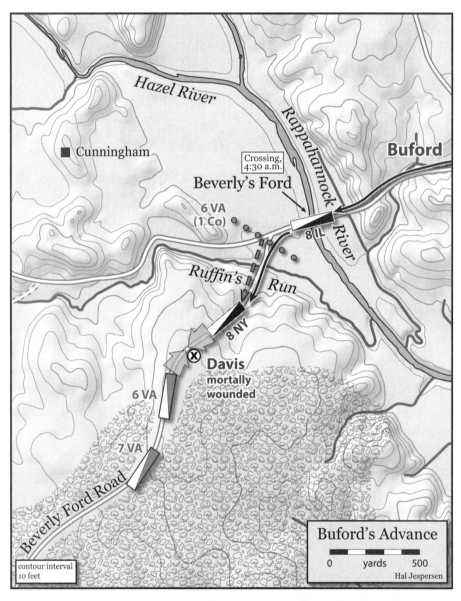

BUFORD'S ADVANCE—In the pre-dawn hours of June 9, 1863, Brig. Gen. John Buford's Union cavalry wing moved to cross the Rappahannock River at Beverly Ford. Buford's movement opened the largest cavalry engagement ever to take place in North America. Despite stiff resistance and the loss of one of his brigade commanders—Col. Benjamin Davis—Buford was able to secure the south bank of the river to allow the remainder of his troopers to cross.

followed by the 8th Illinois and 3rd Indiana. Waiting for the Yankees were pickets from the 6th Virginia Cavalry, who gave them a warm reception. One New Yorker recalled that they were greeted with a "sharp fire from the enemy's rifle pits."

Firing from a barricade rails, one of the first Virginia volleys struck Lt. Henry Clay Cutler, the 23-year-old commander of Co. B of the 8th New York Cavalry. Angered by his loss, the New Yorkers charged and scattered the enemy picket line.

Still, the Confederates withdrew slowly, using the ditches on either side of the Beverly Ford Road as protection, thereby preventing the Union troopers from flanking them. Their action bought time for Maj. Cabell E. Flournoy to assemble 150 men of the 6th Virginia Cavalry to blunt the Union onslaught.

"There being no information or apprehension of an attack, our men had, carelessly, turned their horses out to graze," remembered a Rebel. The Union charge caught many of the Confederates asleep or cooking breakfast. "The Company was surprised," one Confederate remembered. Catching the enemy off guard, Davis' advance continued. The Union column bore down on the Confederate horse artillery parked there. If the Federals could capture the guns, they could seriously neutralize Stuart's combat effectiveness.

Fortuitously and despite the confusion in the ranks, Flournoy mounted a desperate countercharge, many of his troopers pitching into the fight without their coats and riding bare back. "We had not gone a quarter of a mile when suddenly a heavy fire was poured into our ranks by their skirmishers who filled the woods on each side of us," one New Yorker remembered. Flournoy's contingent struck Davis in the middle of

From the Confederate Artillery Park looking toward the Rappahannock, the line of trees to the right marks the Beverly Ford Road. (dd)

Despite lacking a formal military education, Col. Thomas Devin proved to be a skillful cavalryman. His superior, John Buford, said, "He knows more about the tactics than I do." (usahec)

Brig. Gen. William "Grumble" Jones rendered invaluable service in saving the Confederate artillery. Although Jones did not get along with J. E. B. Stuart, the cavalry commander begrudgingly called him "the best outpost officer in the army." (loc)

the road. For a few brief moments, the two sides fired pistols and sliced at each other with sabers at close quarters. The charge was critical and "of great value." It allowed the Confederate horse artillery to withdraw to the safety of the next ridge, where St. James Church stood.

With Flournoy's men retreating, Grimes Davis found himself alone, at the head of his column in the middle of the road. Turning to his men, he yelled, "Stand firm, Eighth New York!" Then, sensing a presence approaching, Davis immediately turned and swung his saber. He missed Lt. Robert Owen Allen of the 6th Virginia. Allen had been at the rear of Flournoy's column and had ridden back to confront Davis. Ducking Davis' saber, Allen fired his pistol. The ball struck Davis in the head; he was dead before his body fell to the ground.

After the battle, Buford proudly wrote that "the success was dearly bought, for among the noble and brave ones who fell was Col. B. F. Davis, 8th N.Y. Cav. He died in the front giving examples of heroism and courage to all who were to follow." To Buford, Davis "was a thorough soldier, free from politics and intrigue, a patriot in its true sense, an ornament to his country and a bright star in his profession."

*   *   *

Awakened by the gunfire, Grumble Jones rushed to the front, bootless, yelling to one officer, "We'll give them Hell!" Other Confederates also joined the fray. The 7th Virginia Cavalry rode to the aid of the 6th Virginia. Making good on Jones' vow, the two regiments counterattacked, striking the 8th Illinois. Knifing into their rear, the Virginians nearly captured three companies, until "part of the Eighth Illinois regiment not engaged in the fight . . . had an opportunity to display their courage, and . . . the enemy were forced to yield the ground, after a bloody encounter."

Major Flournoy was once more in the thick of the fight, engaging the Illinois commander, Capt. Alpheus Clark, whom Flournoy shot in the hand. Captain George Forsyth took over for Clark, who later died of lead poisoning as a result of the wound. Forsyth himself was also wounded during the fighting, meaning that regimental command devolved to the

promising Capt. Elon J. Farnsworth, who skillfully directed the regiment for the remainder of the day.

News of the fighting soon reached Stuart's headquarters on Fleetwood Hill. Gleefully, Capt. William Farley, Stuart's favorite scout, shouted, "Hurrah! We're going to have a fight!" Swinging into action, Stuart, followed by his aides, rode off toward the sound of the firing. Galloping toward the wooden St. James Episcopal Church, Stuart took command of the field and quickly assessed the situation.

Although the Union attack came as a surprise, Stuart had to be pleased with what he saw. His troopers, along with his horse artillery, had gradually fallen back to the ridge occupied by St. James Church. The ridge itself extended west of the Beverly Ford Road. To the east was a knoll upon which stood the modest brick house of Emily Gee. Stuart's presence further seemed to bring order to a chaotic situation. Also arriving on the field was Rooney Lee's brigade, who took up a position off Jones' left flank.

Upon hearing of Davis' death, Buford crossed the river, bringing with him reinforcements. His first task was to throw the 3rd Indiana—whose commander, Maj. William McClure, succeeded Davis—into the fight. Buford also deployed the Reserve Brigade and Ames' infantry brigade.

Also coming onto the field was Col. Thomas C. Devin's Second Brigade, which followed the First. "[A]s Colonel Devin approached the skirmish

In desperation, the gray cannoneers managed to evacuate their guns from this field and back to the new line at St. James Church. (cm)

Benjamin Franklin "Grimes" Davis was a Southerner and first cousin of Confederate President Jefferson Davis. Rather than siding with the South, Davis chose to fight for the United States. During the Maryland Campaign, he led a daring cavalry escape from the encircled garrison at Harper's Ferry. "When Colonel Davis found the rebels he did not stop at anything, but went for them heavy," one of his troopers said of him. "I believe he liked to fight the rebels as well as he liked to eat." (usahec)

line, he at once became the target for the Rebel sharpshooters," a trooper in the 17th Pennsylvania Cavalry recalled. "[I]t was the next thing to a miracle that he was not killed." A few moments later, his horse was shot out from under him.

With more Federals coming onto the field, Grumble Jones decided to commit the last of his reserves to the fight. In an effort to secure his flanks and rear, Jones sent the 11th and 12th Virginia regiments, along with the troopers of the 35th Battalion of Virginia Cavalry, to St. James Church. Rather than waiting for them to deploy, the aggressive Jones instead ordered them to charge.

"It was . . . hand to hand . . . killing, wounding, and taking prisoners promiscuously," recalled a trooper in the 12th Virginia. Charles O'Ferrall, a captain and future governor of Virginia, led his squadron of the 12th Virginia into the action. The Federals unleashed a devastating volley and then countercharged. The 12th Virginia's colonel, Asher Harman, then ordered the rest of the regiment to go to O'Ferrall's support. Falling back, the Virginians then counterattacked. The seesaw fight was "close . . . and furious," with both blue and gray sustaining heavy losses. While the 12th Virginia was engaged, the 35th Battalion of Virginia Cavalry engaged in a similar fight near the Gee house. Their attack, initially successful, was eventually driven back by the Union troopers. Fortunately for the Confederates, more help was on the way.

"As soon as the firing was heard, 'boots and saddles' was sounded, and our brigade hurried forward," wrote a trooper from the Cobb Legion Cavalry of Brig. Gen. Wade Hampton's brigade.

The South Carolinian quickly rode to Stuart's aid. Hampton deployed sharpshooters along the Beverly Ford Road while extending the line east from the Gee house. One of his officers recalled that "they charged the Yankees and drove them through the woods . . . our men . . . expended nearly all their ammunition."

Despite the initial shock of the enemy incursion, and after three hours of fighting, Stuart had managed to blunt Buford's offensive. Hampton's added weight gave Stuart a second brigade along the ridge at St. James Church from which to further contest any Union advance.

They did not have long to wait: Buford intended to test that line's mettle.

Standing with cavalry commander Alfred Pleasonton, George Armstrong Custer (left) participated in the opening phases of the battle. (loc)

To the Artillery Park

You are now in the area where skirmishers from the 8th New York first made contact with pickets from the 6th Virginia Cavalry. Turn around and retrace your route along the Beverly Ford Road. You are following the advance of Grimes Davis's brigade after they crossed the Rappahannock. A trooper from the 6th Virginia remembered that as his comrades withdrew before Davis' advance, "the fight was at close quarters, and for a short time was fierce and bloody." During their delaying action, the Virginians lost 20 percent of their total force engaged.

In 0.7 miles you will reach a sharp bend in the road to the right. Lieutenant Robert Allen killed Grimes Davis here.

Accompanying Davis's brigade was a young captain on Pleasonton's staff, George Armstrong Custer.

Davis's and Jones's troopers fought for control of this ground in the early stages of the fighting. (cm)

Impressed with Custer's actions, Pleasonton later that day sent him to present the captured battle flag of the 12th Virginia to Joseph Hooker.

In 0.2 miles, turn right into the parking lot. This is tour stop 3. Note the road that parallels the tree line, which is the driveway to Tour Stop 5 that follows the battle in Chapter 6.

You are now standing in the area of the encampment of Stuart's Horse Artillery, commanded by Maj. Robert F. Beckham, a native of Culpeper County. Moving the guns to safety was a key action in the opening stages of the battle. To help cover their withdrawal, Capt. James F. Hart of the Washington (South Carolina) Artillery deployed two pieces in the Beverly Ford Road and engaged the Union cavalry. Supporting Flournoy's charge, Hart engaged the advancing cavalry and bought time for the Confederate batteries to withdraw to safety on the new line along the ridge at St. James Church. When the Federal horsemen approached too close, the artillerists engaged them with their

After fording the Rappahannock, Davis's troopers had to cross Ruffan's Run as they continued the advance. (dd)

rammers. Hart, with his guns, was eventually able to withdraw to the new line. Despite the proximity of so many Yankees, the Confederates only lost Major Beckham's field desk.

There are trails here with interpretive signs that discuss the opening phases of the battle.

GPS: 38° 31.979′N, 77° 51.464′W

━━━➤ **TO STOP 4**

Turn right and proceed 0.8 miles, then turn right onto St. James Church Road. Bear to your left into the parking lot. Get out of your vehicle and walk to the end of the parking lot.

GPS: 38° 31.293′N, 77° 51.939′W

A Charge of Conspicuous Gallantry

CHAPTER FIVE

With his First Division across the river, Alfred Pleasonton sent a missive to Washington regarding the situation. "The enemy is in strong cavalry force," declared Pleasonton. "We have had a severe fight."

As his chief was writing to his superiors, John Buford rode to the top of a knoll just north of the Beverly Ford Road, where he established his headquarters. Deploying Lt. Samuel Elder's battery atop the high ground, the division commander had a full view of the battlefield. Buford, however, did not have a good idea of the force directly in front of him. The Confederate cavalry had rallied and Buford wanted to know exactly what he was facing.

Deciding to probe the Rebel lines, Buford sent an order to Maj. Robert Morris, Jr., the commander of the 6th Pennsylvania Cavalry. Buford directed Morris "to clear the woods in his front." Morris' five companies looked out across a field nearly half a mile wide, intersected by four ditches. The ground rose steadily to the woods and the St. James Church ridge where Stuart's troopers and 16 artillery pieces awaited them.

Forming in line of battle, Morris' troopers began their advance. They made a "dash of conspicuous gallantry" across the wide meadow. The regiment "charged the enemy home, riding almost up to the mouths of his cannon," nearly capturing two of the

Rough-hewn pews stand today within the marked foundation of St. James Church. (cm)

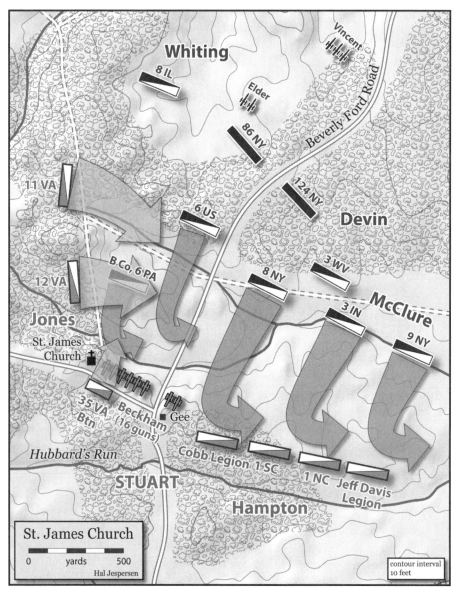

Sт. James Church—**After Buford's initial advance across Beverly Ford, the Confederates were able to establish a makeshift line near St. James Church. There, Stuart stabilized his position and repulsed a major attack by the 6th Pennsylvania Cavalry. Stuart's success was short-lived: reports began to arrive about Union cavalry appearing in his rear in Brandy Station.**

Confederate guns. "Shells burst over us, under us, and alongside," remembered one trooper, "and bullets were singing through the air like a hornet's nest."

Major Henry Whelan remembered the troopers "dashed at them, squadron front with drawn sabres, and as we flew along-our men yelling like demons-

grape and cannister were poured into our left flank and a storm of rifle bullets on our front."

> We had to leap three wide deep ditches, and many of our horses and men piled up in a writhing mass in those ditches and were ridden over. It was here that Maj. Morris's horse fell badly with him, and broke away from him when he got up, thus leaving him dismounted and bruised by the fall. I didn't know that Morris was not with us, and we dashed on, driving the Rebels into and through the woods, our men fighting with the sabre alone, whilst they used principally pistols. Our brave fellows cut them out of the saddle and fought like tigers, until I discovered they were on both flanks, pouring a cross fire of carbines and pistols on us, and then tried to rally my men and make them return the fire with their carbines.

Recklessly joining the charge was Capt. Ulric Dahlgren. Two days before, Dahlgren, who served on Maj. Gen. Joseph Hooker's staff, had been sent from army headquarters with the orders for Pleasonton to conduct this expedition. Per his orders, the daring and ambitious 21-year-old captain then accompanied the expedition.

Alfred Waud witnessed the 6th Pennsylvania's charge and later sketched it for *Harper's Weekly*. The Emily Gee House can be seen at the top left center of the drawing. (loc)

The 6th Pennsylvania launched their charge against this location. The charge began near the wood line at the far left corner of the distant field. (cm)

Dahlgren rode next to Major Morris during the charge. "Just as we were jumping a ditch," Dahlgren wrote, "some canister came along, and I saw his horse fall over him, but could not tell whether he was killed or not, for at the same instant my horse was shot in three places." The wounded horse fell, throwing him. "Just then the column turned to go back,—finding that the enemy had surrounded us," Dahlgren recounted. "I saw the rear passing me, and about to leave me behind, so I gave my horse a tremendous kick and got him on his legs again. Finding he could still move, I mounted and made after the rest,—just escaping being taken. I got a heavy blow over the arm from the back of a saber, which bruised me somewhat, and nearly unhorsed me." The brave young man rallied the Pennsylvanians and led them to safety.

"When within two hundred yards of us and the guns about to use canister, Lt. Col. Elijah V. White, commanding a small detachment of Virginia cavalry, led his force between our guns and the enemy," wrote one artillerist, "and gallantly charged into them. Our fire ceased instantly, and with nothing else in their way, the charging column rolled back White's little

force as if it was a wisp of straw and thundered on . . . the guns, doubled shotted with canister . . . delivered their last fire into the mass of Federals and Virginians alike, but it was now too late to stop them." The attack was "one of the most daring charges the cavalry on either side had attempted up to this time."

Captain James Hart, whose gallant actions helped save the very guns that were now dealing death and destruction, wrote, "Never rode troopers more gallantly than those steady Regulars, as under a fire of shell and shrapnel, and finally of canister, they dashed up to the very muzzles."

The historian of the Army of Northern Virginia's artillery branch, Jennings Cropper Wise, remembered that "the Light Brigade's charge at Balaclava was no more daring than the one which [the Federals made] at Saint James Church, the latter possessing the additional feature that it was premeditated and not the result of accident."

One Pennsylvania trooper recalled "what an awful fire! So close that we are almost in the smoke of the battery. Many of our saddles are emptied . . . and at the same moment, hundreds of carbines fend their charges of death into our never-wavering ranks."

The 6th Pennsylvania began their charge from the corner of the field at left center, moving parallel to St. James Church Road. Confederates appeared on the Federal flank, along the left side of the road, and poured enfilading fire into the horsemen, who also took direct fire from Confederate artillery. (cm)

The **Emily Gee House stood on this knoll on the other side of the Beverly Ford Road. As the Confederate line at St. James Church took shape, Wade Hampton deployed his brigade on the opposite side of the knoll.** (cm)

Particularly, he noted the loss of the men who carried the regimental flag. "Our color sergeant reels, and from his horse; another sergeant catches the colors before they reach the ground; and on through the storm of death our weakened lines advance until they meet the enemy, and hand to hand the conflict rages."

Sustaining a withering fire, the five companies of the 6th Pennsylvania were in trouble. Their thinned ranks left them vulnerable to a counterattack.

Lieutenants Louis H. Carpenter and Andrew Stoll of the 6th U.S. Cavalry watched the attack of the gallant Keystoners. At the head of four squadrons, Carpenter and Stoll launched a charge of their own to cover the withdrawal of Morris' men. Carpenter wrote, "As we went along at headlong speed, cheering . . . the air was perfectly filled with bullets and pieces of shell, shells burst over us, under us, and alongside."

The squadrons reached the field as Jones' Virginians counterattacked. Caught in the melee, "hundreds of glittering sabres instantly leaped from their scabbards, gleamed and flashed in the morning sun . . . while hundreds of little puffs of white smoke gracefully rose through the balmy June air from discharging firearms all over the field in front of our batteries."

The squadrons of the 6th U.S. provided a devastating fire that helped cover the retreat of the Pennsylvanians. At times receiving cannon blasts at a distance of 50 yards, the two regiments withdrew back to their own lines. To assist them, Buford directed Elder's battery to open fire. Covered by the topography, many of Elder's shells missed their counterparts and instead landed in the ranks of the gray cavalry.

While the 6th Pennsylvania and the 6th U.S. probed Stuart's line, Buford moved the 17th Pennsylvania and 6th New York of Devin's brigade, along with a section from Capt. William Graham's Battery K, 1st U.S. Artillery, to shore up his northern flank. He now held a position opposite that of St. James Church that spread from the Rappahannock on his left across the farm of Richard Hoopes Cunningham to the Hazel River, a tributary of the Rappahannock, on his right.

In extending the line, Devin ran into elements of the 11th Virginia and the 35th Virginia Battalion that Jones had dispatched. The Northerners collided with the Confederates, who eventually gained the upper hand and shoved Devin's men back. Determined to regain the ground lost, Devin moved forward in a dismounted line of battle and counterattacked, driving Jones' troopers back to St. James Church. For a time, the fighting was close and bloody.

Hampton's troopers also pitched into the fight with Devin. A North Carolinian wrote after the battle, "Our regiment, the 1st North Carolina, along with

Following the initial Union assault, Stuart established a new position along this ridge. (cm)

the Jeff Davis Legion were deployed . . . fighting the enemy with good success, driving them back on their reserves." Stalled, Hampton attempted to turn Devin's line, but the Empire Stater held firm.

With both sides at loggerheads on the St. James Church front, the axis of the fighting shifted from the center of the battle lines to the left and a lonely stone wall along the Cunningham farm.

At St. James Church Ridge

A sign marks the beginning of a trail that leads to the site of St. James Church and its cemetery. (cm)

You are now standing in the Confederate line that was established following the initial stages of the battle. To your right on the knoll on the far side of the Beverly Ford Road stood the Emily Gee house. Pleaston set up his headquarters here during the later stages of the engagement. As the battle developed, Wade Hampton's brigade occupied the other side of the knoll beyond the house.

The trail and interpretive markers discuss the fighting that took place in this area during the battle. The 6th Pennsylvania Cavalry began its desperate charge in the distant tree line across the field. At one point, the Pennsylvanians penetrated the Rebel line in the vicinity in which you are now standing. A Confederate artillerist on the firing line recalled that as the Keystoners approached, his battery "gave them fifty rounds" and that the battle for the guns was "fearful hard work."

Turn to your left and walk down the road toward the site of St. James Church. When you reach the sign, follow the trail into the woods. The church itself was 40 by 40 feet wide and was two stories tall, built of red brick with a wooden frame. In 1860, the congregation consisted of 28 individuals. Blacks attended services and sat in the gallery, while whites sat below. In late 1863, as the Army of the Potomac settled its winter encampment near Brandy Station, the 6th U.S. Cavalry, which fought in the fields in front of the church during the battle, demolished

the building in order to use the wood and brick to construct their living quarters. The church was later rebuilt in a different location.

The church cemetery is beyond the outline of the church. Only a few markers and headstones remain, one to an unknown artillerist from the famed Washington Artillery of New Orleans, who may have been killed during a skirmish along the Rappahannock River during the Second Manassas campaign in August 1862. The dips in the ground surrounding you are unmarked graves.

While a few headstones still rise above the groundcover, many of the graves in the St. James Church Cemetery are unmarked, visible only as depressions in the ground. (cm)

⟶ **TO STOP 5**

Return to Tour Stop 3, the Confederate Artillery Park, and follow the drive that parallels the tree line .75 miles and park.

GPS: 38° 32.592′N, 77° 51.509′W

Located at the far edge of the cemetery is an unknown artillerist from the Washington Artillery of New Orleans. Formed as an Antebellum militia unit, the Artillery fielded batteries that served in both the Eastern and Western Confederate armies. (cm)

To the Stone Wall

CHAPTER SIX

As Buford tested the line at St. James Church, Rooney Lee's troopers readied themselves to enter the fight. Earlier that morning, without orders to do so, and responding to the crisis unfolding in front of him, Lee brought his men to the aid of Jones, deploying to his left. Lee's men took position behind an L-shaped stone wall on the Richard Cunningham farm, where they could hear the Union attacks to their right. Rising directly behind the Confederates was a northern extension of Fleetwood Hill, Yew Ridge. A strong defensive position, it offered Lee the opportunity to potentially enfilade the enemy line.

With Federal skirmishers in his immediate front, Lee sent forward dismounted sharpshooters to clear them out and secure the area. Sallying forth, members of the 9th Virginia moved out to engage the enemy. "After advancing . . . about 1/2 mile the fire became general," one Confederate wrote. "Along the line there was an incessant roar of small arms which lasted all day."

This movement, in turn, stirred up the 5th U.S. Cavalry. Engaging Lee's troopers, the Regulars briefly captured a portion of the wall before finally being driven back. This temporary success inspired Buford, who decided to send the rest of the Reserve Brigade into the fight. These soldiers joined the brigades of Maj. William McClure and Col. Thomas Devin on the firing line. Brigadier General Adelbert Ames' supporting infantry brigade formed on the cavalry's flanks.

In conjunction with the deployment, Lieutenant

This high knoll served as John Buford's headquarters and command post. From its crest, Buford directed the fighting against the St. James Church line, the Cunningham Farm, and Yew Ridge. (cm)

Elder's artillery engaged the Confederates. This artillery duel grew in ferocity, paving the way for Buford's men to attack the stone wall once again. Firing from their sheltered position, Lee's men blasted the Yankees and turned back their assault once again.

Rooney Lee's troopers deployed behind the stone wall to blunt Buford's initial advance. The Confederates held their position and kept the Yankees at bay for most of the battle. (cm)

The 124th New York Infantry came up in support of the cavalry. Arriving about the same time as their comrades' retreat, one man remembered that the "wounded . . . began to straggle back past us . . . some of these were on horseback, others with pale faces and blood-stained   garments came staggering along on foot, and occasionally one was borne hurriedly by on a stretcher . . . a little farther on we began to pass over, and saw lying on either side of us, lifeless bodies of men, dressed, some in grey and some in blue."

Known as the "Orange Blossoms," the New Yorkers found themselves in a band of thick woods with an open field to their front. Forming in a single line of battle, the Union infantry were directed to defend their position. Anxiously, they watched as dismounted Rebel cavalry entered a ravine and began working their way around the flank of the Union line. Opening fire, the Confederates then charged the New Yorkers who returned their volley. This firefight soon escalated into one called "a hand to hand Indian fight." Seeing the plight of their fellow Empire Staters, a company of the 86th New York came to the aid of the 124th New York. The arrival of the reinforcements drove back the Confederates. Shouted orders from men on horseback hastened the withdrawal of the Confederates, who believed that a mounted Union charge was about to befall them, the Rebels gave up the fight. Interestingly, those hollered commands came from the colonel of the 124th New York, Augustus Van Horne Ellis, and several members of his staff. Their ruse helped beat back the attack.

This brisk action prompted Ames to dispatch companies from the 3rd Wisconsin and 2nd Massachusetts Infantry to the aid of the New Yorkers as well as to support Devin. A Wisconsin soldier remembered, "soon the infantry were at business" and in the middle of "a lively fight."

While his infantry reinforcements forced the Confederates back, Ames decided to add more of his infantry to the fight. He decided to send in soldiers from his Bay State regiments. Supported by the 2nd Massachusetts, the 33rd Massachusetts advanced. One soldier remembered that their "skirmishers so annoyed a rebel battery at the edge of the woods beyond."

In response to the infantry threat, Stuart redoubled his artillery efforts and ordered Beckham to concentrate on the foot soldiers. Along with Beckham's fire, the Confederate commander advanced sharpshooters and shifted part of Lee's brigade to support them. The action escalated into a slugfest. Even with the added weight of the enemy infantry attacking his line, Stuart held firm. One Indiana trooper remembered, "Both parties fought earnestly and up to 12 o'clock the enemy held his position."

A lull soon settled over the field. As both sides attempted to recover and evacuate their wounded, Stuart prepared for a counterattack. However, it soon became obvious that his plans might all be for naught. Around 11:30, a trooper from the 8th New York wrote that he could "hear the booming of distant cannon . . . . Gen. Graig (sic) had arrived . . . and was engaging the enemy." The guns reached the ears of John Buford at his headquarters. Although Buford had been on his own for nearly six hours, from his perspective, the fight was far from over. He "resolved to go to him if possible."

Unfortunately, Alfred Pleasonton did not possess the gritty determination of Buford. As Gregg's division arrived on the field, Pleasonton sent a dispatch to Hooker stating "all the enemy's force are engaged with me. I am holding them until Gregg can come up. Gregg's guns are being heard in the enemy's rear." Stuart's stubborn defense took the starch out of Pleasonton, who cautiously held Buford in check, refusing to allow the frustrated Kentuckian to advance.

The surprise that Stuart received earlier in the morning paled in comparison to the shock he was about to experience. A new phase of the fighting was about to erupt in his rear along Fleetwood Hill.

At Buford's Knoll

The imminence before you is Buford's Knoll. Buford's Knoll may only be accessible seasonally. There is no paved parking, so please use caution.

Here, John Buford established his headquarters after he crossed the river and directed the battle. Pull your car around, park and follow the trail to the interpretive signs on the crest of the knoll. Directly behind you was the position of Battery E, 4th U.S. Artillery, under Lt. Samuel Elder. To your immediate left front and hidden by the tree lines is the site of St. James Church. The stone wall that Rooney Lee deployed his troopers behind on the Cunningham farm is in the tree line directly to your front and below you. The high ground beyond is Yew Ridge (the action here is described in Chapter 9).

You may walk to the stone wall by following the trail that parallels the tree line in the area where you parked. Due to heavy vegetation and snakes, it is recommended that you only walk to the site during the fall, winter, and early spring. Continue along the trail until the woods turn to your right. Follow the path into the woods and you will find the stone wall.

GPS: 38° 32.592′N, 77° 51.509′W

At the Stone Wall

In 1863, the wall was about waist high. During the morning fight for the stone wall, Capt. James E. Harrison of the 5th U.S. Cavalry led two squadrons in an assault on Lee's position. Thirty-one years old, Harrison, a Virginian, had remained loyal to the Old Flag when his native state seceded in 1861. Fighting dismounted, Harrison led his troopers in an assault on the wall. The fighting here was bitter. Although heavily outnumbered, the Regulars were able to capture a portion of the wall and hold it against several counterattacks. It was only when his men ran out of ammunition that Harrison ordered a withdrawal. The 5th U.S. sustained 38 casualties during the engagement here, including four killed and three mortally wounded.

Although overgrown in many areas, the stone wall on the Cunningham Farm, occupied by Rooney Lee's troopers throughout the battle, still stands today. (cm)

If you wish to have more details about the action that occurred here and on Yew Ridge directly in rear of the stone wall, you may turn to Chapter 9. Otherwise, return to your vehicle. Drive back to the Beverly Ford Road and turn right.

→ **TO STOP 6**

Turn right on the Beverly Ford. In 1.2 miles, bear right onto Cobb's Legion Lane and follow it to the stop sign. Turn right onto Fleetwood Heights Road. In 0.8 miles, you will pass the United Daughters of the Confederacy marker on your left. As you crest the hill, you will see a parking area and a Civil War Trust sign on your left. You will return to this site in the next chapter. Proceed over the crest of Fleetwood Hill. Travelling 0.4 miles beyond the marker, you will see a pull off on the left with interpretive signs. Pull in, get out of your vehicle, and face Fleetwood Hill.

GPS: 38° 30.45' N, 77° 53' W

Gregg's Arrival

CHAPTER SEVEN

The troopers of Brig. Gen. David Gregg's division had spent the early morning hours anxiously awaiting their turn to cross the Rappahannock at Kelly's Ford. Their delay came in the form of Col. Alfred Duffié's division, which was to join them after marching from Warrenton. Much to Gregg's chagrin, Duffié took a wrong turn during the march and thus arrived three hours behind schedule. By the time he reached the ford, Gregg's men were in the saddle, "the thunder of Buford's cannon, borne on the calm morning air from Beverly Ford" echoing in the distance.

Preceding the cavalry across the ford were elements of Brig. Gen. David Russell's infantry brigade. Russell's assignment was to move across the river and secure the crossing for the cavalry and keep it open for their eventual return.

Guarding the river was a brigade of North Carolinians, two large and experienced regiments commanded by Brig. Gen. Beverly H. Robertson. On Russell's order, a detail from the 5th New Hampshire Infantry, supported by a detachment from the 81st Pennsylvania, stormed through the water and up the opposite bank. Exchanging several shots with the Tar Heels, the New Hampshire men quickly seized control of the ford and drove away the Confederate pickets, securing Kelly's Ford for both the initial crossing and for the cavalry's eventual return.

The first horsemen to cross were Capt. P. Jones Yorke and his squadron of the 1st New Jersey Cavalry.

This view greeted David Gregg as he deployed his brigades to assault Fleetwood Hill. (dd)

An experienced infantry officer and veteran of the Mexican War, Brig. Gen. David Russell's brigade sustained heavy losses at the battle of Chancellorsville. (loc)

A cousin of the wartime governor of Pennsylvania, Andrew Curtain, Brig. Gen. David Gregg (above) was an accomplished cavalryman. His service during the Peninsula and Maryland Campaigns had earned him his brigadier's stars by the end of 1862. (loc)

Similar to the infantry's experience, Yorke's Jerseymen also captured a number of the North Carolina pickets.

Gregg, like Buford, was surprised to find Confederates at Kelly's Ford—a result of Pleasonton's faulty assumptions. Fortunately for Gregg, his men captured the enemy videttes before they could spread the alarm.

Around 6 a.m., the column began crossing. For some three hours, Gregg and Duffié sloshed across the river. By the time both divisions were on the south bank, Buford had been engaged for almost five hours. All the while, the troopers could hear the fighting raging around St. James Church. One trooper recalled that many of the men around him "tightened the girth of his saddle, and examined his carbine, and tried the edge of his sabre on the ball of his thumb."

*   *   *

Word of the presence of the Union cavalry made its way up the chain of command to Robertson and finally to Stuart. Stuart, in turn, directed Robertson to engage the Yankees at Kelly's Ford and to cover the Confederate right. Riding toward the Ford, Robertson found some of his troopers in the vicinity of John Kelly's mill. Robertson slowly withdrew before the enemy advance. When Russell's infantry appeared in their front, Robertson decided to turn and hold them in check with dismounted skirmishers. Along with the skirmishers, scouts went out on Robertson's right. They returned with disheartening news.

Gregg's division, the scouts said, had already moved around Robertson's right flank and were headed to Brandy Station. Robertson immediately sent a galloper to Stuart to inform him of this development. Shortly after the first courier left, word arrived that Duffié had also eluded the Confederates and was riding toward Stevensburg, prompting another galloper to head off.

Robertson later wrote that Stuart ordered him to retreat and join him on Fleetwood Hill, leaving the road to Brandy Station unguarded. Stuart quickly changed his mind and ordered Robertson to take up a position along the Kelly's Mill Road position to block the Federal advance. The Confederates, however, occupied a road that was not used by Gregg. Instead, Robertson blocked the route of Russell's infantry

KELLY'S FORD

At this site in 1863 the
federal forces charged
across the river to begin
the Battle of Kelly's Ford &
Brandy Station. Traces of
the ford & John P. Kelly's
toll, 1837 to 1862, may
still be seen at this spot.

advance, which Pleasonton had envisioned moving on Brandy Station after the river crossing.

The Tar Heels engaged Russell for several hours. Then the Union commander ordered up his artillery and opened fire, prompting the North Carolinians to withdraw. One soldier in blue wrote, "They ran away after a little skirmish."

Beverly Robertson put forth little effort to block the Federals. Irate, Stuart wrote afterwards, "Brigadier-General Robertson kept the enemy in check . . . but did not conform to the movement of the enemy . . . of which he was cognizant . . . to hold him in check or thwart him by a corresponding move . . . in the same direction. He was too far off for me to give him orders to do so in time."

The North Carolinians skirmished lightly with Russell for the remainder of the day until Robertson finally received orders to join Stuart at Brandy Station. However, Robertson did not arrive until the battle was over. His casualties that day amounted to four horses killed.

Gregg's and Duffie's divisions crossed the Rappahannock here. The ford is located downstream from the modern bridge. (cm)

* * *

Union troopers from Maryland and Pennsylvania advanced across this field during their attack on Fleetwood Hill. (dd)

While Russell kept Robertson occupied, Gregg's division rode toward Brandy Station. "We galloped through the woods over a road so dusty that we could hardly recognize each other," a Maine trooper recalled.

With the guns booming at St. James Church, Gregg oddly took a longer route than necessary to reach his destination, allowing Stuart to continue to batter Buford. For a time, Gregg proceeded along the Fredericksburg Plank Road, which effectively added three additional miles to the march. Soon, a courier arrived from Pleasonton notifying Gregg "of the severity of the fight." After ordering Duffié to Brandy Station, Gregg turned his division in that direction.

A reporter with the New York Times wrote that the Union troopers rode over terrain that was "rolling, interspersed with clumps of trees, and not the most desirable for cavalry operations." Despite the obstacles, he remembered the Federals kept "in excellent order."

While still holding the line at St. James Church, Grumble Jones learned of Gregg's advance and sent a courier to warn Stuart. After hearing the courier's report, Stuart scoffed, "Tell Gen. Jones to attend to the Yankees in his front, and I'll watch the flanks." When informed of his chief's response, Jones angrily replied, "So he thinks they ain't coming, does he? Well, let him alone; he'll damned well soon see for himself."

Once upon a time, this was the view from the area where the modern wayside signs now stand. A private "McMansion"-style home sat on the crest of Fleetwood Hill, and the owner built a private lake at the hill's base. The property became an iconic symbol in the battle to preserve Brandy Station. For more on the preservation story, see the Afterword by O. James Lighthizer, president of the Civil War Trust. (ew)

At the Base of Fleetwood Hill

You now have a view of what awaited Gregg when he reached Brandy Station, which is directly behind you and across 15/29. About three quarters of a mile before reaching Brandy Station, Gregg formed his division for the coming engagement. Deploying his two brigades into three columns each, Col. Percy Wyndham occupied the left while Col. Judson Kilpatrick held the right of Gregg's line.

Around 11 a.m., Wyndham arrived near the tracks of the Orange & Alexandria Railroad. There, he sighted a single cannon on Fleetwood Hill directly to your front. If Gregg could seize the high ground, Stuart would be trapped between his division and Buford.

⟶ TO STOP 7

Return to your vehicle, cautiously enter the road, and return to the parking lot at the top of Fleetwood Hill. Pull into the lot and get out of your vehicle. There is a trail here with interpretive markers.

GPS: 38° 50.963′ N, 77° 87.975′ W

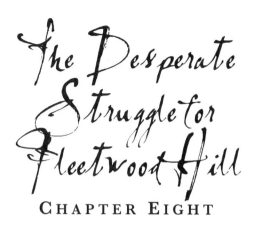

The Desperate Struggle for Fleetwood Hill

CHAPTER EIGHT

Stuart's adjutant, Maj. Henry B. McClellan, was standing on Fleetwood Hill a few minutes before 11:30. A newcomer to Stuart's staff, McClellan was a native Philadelphian who had attended Williams College and, after graduating, settled in Cumberland County, Virginia. He was working as a schoolteacher when war broke out in 1861 and stuck with his adopted state, although four of his brothers served in the Union army, as did his first cousin, Union Maj. Gen. George McClellan.

Major McClellan had just heard the report of Robertson's breathless couriers when Gregg's column appeared before him, headed toward Brandy Station.

"They were pressing steadily toward the railroad station," McClellan recalled. "How could they be prevented from also occupying the Fleetwood Hill, the key to the whole position? Matters looked serious!"

The prominent hill, which dominated the landscape and was only occupied by a few other orderlies, lay open to the Federal assault.

Nearby, however, a 12-pound Napoleon of Capt. Roger P. Chew's Battery, commanded by Lt. John W. "Tuck" Carter, was resupplying its ammunition. Reacting swiftly, McClellan ordered Carter to open on the Yankees while "courier after courier was dispatched to General Stuart to inform him of the peril."

"The Yankees are at Brandy!" yelled the riders as they raced up to Stuart at St. James Church. Immediately,

A marker stands today in the vicinity of Stuart's Headquarters, erected by the United Daughters of the Confederacy in 1926. (cm)

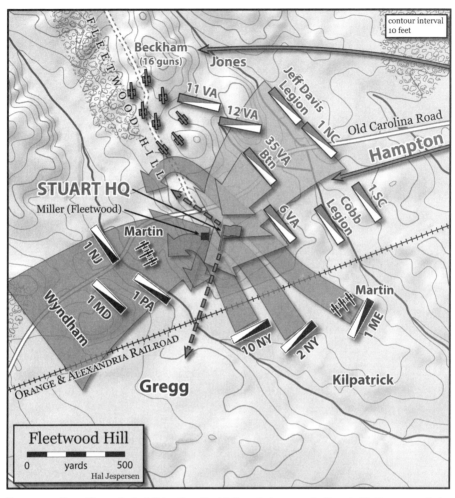

FLEETWOOD HILL—The arrival of Brig. Gen. David Gregg's troopers in Brandy Station presented a severe threat to Stuart's lines at St. James Church. In peril, Stuart rushed men to defend Fleetwood Hill, the rear of his position. This resulted in a heavy see-saw melee across the heights. Stuart was able to hold on and repulse Gregg's attack.

Stuart dispatched the 12th Virginia Cavalry and the 35th Battalion of Virginia Cavalry of Jones' brigade to go to McClellan. "Go for Hampton," Stuart said to one of his staff officers, "Tell him to come. For God's sake, bring Hampton."

Leaving his skirmishers as well as Rooney Lee's brigade to contend with Buford, Stuart pulled Jones' brigade and Hart's battery out of line and dashed to Fleetwood Hill.

Stuart's order reached Hampton, whose brigade began galloping to McClellan's aid with the Cobb Legion Cavalry in the lead. One Confederate staff officer fondly recalled, "No more brilliant spectacle

was ever witnessed than the brave Hampton leading on his gallant Carolinians."

Gregg's troopers neared the crest of the hill just as the Confederate horsemen reached the scene. "There now followed a passage of arms filled with romantic interest and splendor to a degree unequaled by anything our war produced," wrote a Confederate. Elements from Jones' brigade collided with the 1st New Jersey of Col. Sir Percy Wyndham's brigade, with the Federals eventually gaining the upper hand. Then the Confederates counterattacked.

A soldier in the 12th Virginia remembered, "Round and round it went; we would break their line on one side, and they would break ours on the other . . . it was pell mell, helter skelter—a yankee and there a rebel—killing, wounding, and taking prisoners." Another Virginian wrote, "we fought them single-handed, by twos, fours, and by squads, just as the circumstances permitted."

Hammered by the enemy counterattack, the stubborn 1st New Jersey still held onto the hill. Surrounded by the Confederates, the Jerseymen had to hack their way. "The fighting was hand to hand and of the most desperate kind," a lieutenant in the

Henry McClellan was in this area atop Fleetwood Hill when he spotted David Gregg's division arriving in Brandy Station. (dd)

Lt. Col. Virgil Broderick led the 1st New Jersey into the fight on Fleetwood Hill. It would be his last battle. (usahec)

Maj. Henry McClellan played a critical role in notifying Stuart of the threat to the rear of his lines, thus securing Fleetwood Hill. (wc)

regiment, Thomas Cox, wrote. The 1st New Jersey lost their commander, Lt. Col. Virgil Brodrick, and his second in command, Maj. John H. Shelmire. One Union officer recalled, "Col. Brodrick fought like a lion. Wherever the fight was the fiercest his voice could be heard cheering on his men, and his revolver and sabre dealing death." Mortally wounded, Broderick was left behind and captured. He died in enemy hands.

During the ensuing retreat, the Federals lost another officer. Colonel Wyndham went down with a severe leg wound. Choosing to remain with his brigade for the time being, he was eventually forced to leave the field.

As the battle swirled around them on Fleetwood Hill, Capt. Joseph Martin's 6th New York Independent Battery deployed to support the troopers along the southwest slope. Martin's guns proved to be an enticing target for Maj. Cabell Flournoy, who ordered his 6th Virginia to draw sabers and charge. One of the Virginians wrote that Martin's men "were the bravest cannoneers that ever followed a gun . . . we shot their men and horses down, they would fight us with their swabs, with but few of them left." A counterattack eventually forced Flournoy's command back.

A soldier of the 1st Pennsylvania recalled the "heavy crash of the meeting columns, and next the clash of sabers." Then came the "rattle of pistol and carbine, mingling with the frenzied imprecation, the wild shriek that follows the death blow, the demand to surrender, and the appeal for mercy, forming the horrid din of battle." One North Carolinian vividly remembered that "the whole plain was covered with men and horses, charging in all directions . . . with banners flying, sabers glittering, and the fierce flash of firearms, amid the din, dust, and smoke of battle . . . such scenes cannot last beyond a few fearful minutes." A Georgian who witnessed the battle wrote, "Thousands of flashing sabers streamed in the sunlight . . . the surging ranks swayed up and down the sides of Fleetwood Hill . . . dense clouds of smoke and dust rose as a curtain to cover the tumultuous and bloody scene."

Martin's guns launched shell after shell into the

General Lee observed part of the battle from the Beauregard house. When the charge of the 1st Maine Cavalry nearly reached the home, Second Corps commander Richard Ewell suggested the Confederate high command could "gather into the house and defend it to the last." (cm)

Confederate ranks. Their fire grew to be too much for Lt. Col. Elijah V. White, who commanded the 35th Virginia Battalion. His troopers were known for their ferocity in battle, which later earned them the sobriquet "Comanches." White turned to his men and ordered them to charge. "With never a halt or a falter the battalion dashed on, scattering the supports and capturing the battery after a desperate fight, in which the artillerymen fought like heroes, with small arms, long after their guns were silenced," recorded the unit's historian.

Some of the Comanches tried to turn the captured guns on the Yankees. The Federals, however, were girding for a counterattack. Two companies of the 1st Maryland Cavalry advanced, forcing White to withdraw. This small melee left most of the battery's horses dead, forcing the pieces to be moved off the field by hand.

While White and the 1st Maryland struggled below him, Stuart received support in the form of batteries commanded by Capts. William McGregor and Roger Chew. One of the artillerists recalled that the fighting was "fearful . . . we . . . made it so warm for their cavalry, they brought two batteries to play on us."

This additional artillery fire prompted Gregg to commit Judson Kilpatrick's brigade to the fight. Kilpatrick in turn ordered the 10th New York Cavalry to draw sabers and charge. "The rebel line that swept down on us came in splendid order," a member of the regiment wrote, "and when the two lines were about to close in, they opened a rapid fire." What

Lt. Col. Elijah White's regiment was involved in one of the better-known episodes of the battle: They charged down Fleetwood Hill to attack the 6th New York Independent Battery. Although they temporarily captured the pieces, an enemy counterattack forced White to withdraw. (loc)

A New Jerseyan and West Point graduate, Col. Judson Kilpatrick was the first Regular Army officer wounded during the war at the battle of Big Bethel. (loc)

occurred next was "an indescribable clashing and slashing, banging and yelling . . . we were . . . fighting desperately to maintain the position."

Brigadier General Wade Hampton's charging horsemen crashed into the 10th New York. Stuart, following along nearby, yelled to the men as they entered the fight, "Give them the sabre, boys!"

Lieutenant Colonel Will Delony of the Cobb Legion remembered, "We moved up at a gallop our Regt in the advance and the enemy ran up two guns on our left flank & we were ordered to charge. . . . I was in the head of the Regt . . . off we went in fine style." With Delony leading one column and their colonel, Pierce M. B. Young, leading another, the Georgians crashed into the Federals. "The day was ours in less time than I can tell it," Deloney wrote. "We pursued them until called off. With the Jeff Davis Legion & one Squadron of the 1st S. C. Regt we drove off the support of their guns."

Colonel John L. Black's 1st South Carolina Cavalry slammed into the 2nd New York Cavalry. The commander of the New Yorkers, Lt. Col. Henry E. Davies, wrote, "By reason of an order improperly given, as is alleged, the head of the column was turned to the left, and proceeded some distance down the railroad." There the South Carolinians struck them. During the ensuing fight, Davies had his horse shot out from under him and received a nasty saber cut that nearly severed his belt but barely missed his body.

The 2nd New York scattered and fled, with Black's regiment storming after them "cutting down the fugitives without mercy." When another of Hampton's regiments threatened their flank, the Empire Staters skedaddled. Kilpatrick, who had previously commanded this regiment and expected a lot from his old command, was furious at their rout.

Attempting to rally his men, Kilpatrick called to the 1st Maine Cavalry—"Men of Maine! You must save the day! Follow me!"—and personally led a charge by the Maine troopers. "The order was received like an electric shock," remembered a Maine officer. "One idea seemed conveyed to every man throughout those squadrons: This is our opportunity come at last! A spirit of emulation seized them." A magnificent sight unfolded as the

Maine men charged. One observer thought, "It was a scene to be witnessed but once in a lifetime."

Their determined charge crashed into the Confederates and saved the Federal guns near Fleetwood Hill.

Wade Hampton's brigade charged across ground inside the tree line in their assault to retain possession of Fleetwood Hill. (dd)

One of Gregg's staff officers attempted to gain assistance in protecting Martin's cannons. Spotting Kilpatrick, he galloped over and asked for help. "To hell with them!" responded Kilpatrick. "Let Gregg look out for his own guns." Shocked, the staffer repeated his request. "No! Damned if I will!" was the reply.

Lieutenant Colonel Charles H. Smith of the 1st Maine ordered some of his men to dismount and fight on foot. One of Smith's officers recalled that he "looked and acted as cool as though on dress parade. As soon as he had rallied his scattered men, he remounted the regiment, formed squadrons and moved directly toward those guns which the enemy had by this time succeeded in loading, and were just in the act of training on the regiment." Just as the Confederate gunners were about to pull the lanyards, Smith turned the column to the right, narrowly avoiding the artillery fire. Smith then gave the order "Fours left into line!" and charged toward the Barbour house.

At one point during the fight, Kilpatrick squared off with one of his old comrades from the U.S. Military Academy at West Point. The two had never liked each other and the war deepened their hatred. The Southerner spotted Kilpatrick, drew his pistol, fired,

Looking south from the Confederate position atop Fleetwood Hill toward Brandy Station (cm)

and missed. "Little Kil," as he was known, drew his saber, and the two officers fenced. "Both men fought like tigers at bay," remembered one soldier who witnessed the duel. Kilpatrick received a slight cut on the arm and slashed back, his injured opponent reeling in the saddle. He then slashed again, killing the Confederate. Riding away, he proclaimed, "That rights a wrong. I have wanted to meet him ever since the war commenced."

The success of Kilpatrick's attack was short lived. As one of Hampton's troopers recalled, "The tide of battle alternated." The Jeff Davis Legion, of Hampton's brigade, attacked east of the railroad tracks, supported by Grumble Jones' hard-fighting regiments. The "fierce struggle" shoved Gregg's division back.

Hampton's troopers bore down on them. Unfortunately, the South Carolinian was unable to drive home the assault. Stuart had ordered two of the South Carolinian's regiments to remain on Fleetwood Hill, so Hampton ordered an assault without his full command. Afterwards, he bitterly complained, "No notice of this disposition of half of my brigade by General Stuart had been given to me by that officer, and I found myself deprived of two of my regiments at the very moment they could have reaped the fruits

Artist Edwin Forbes drew this sketch of the battle of Brandy Station. The mounted fighting was typical of that which occurred for Fleetwood Hill. (loc)

of the victory." Fuming, Hampton watched Gregg withdraw from the field unhindered.

The Federals, however, had left a section of Lt. Wade Wilson's battery of horse artillery about 100 yards north of the railroad tracks. Kilpatrick had ordered Wilson to limber up and follow the rest of the column. Before they could do so, Col. Lunsford L. Lomax's 11th Virginia Cavalry pounced on them "like a whirlwind." Crashing into the guns, Lomax's men engaged the dismounted troopers who were supporting Wilson. These dismounted cavalrymen held off the Rebels long enough for the artillerists to carry their guns off to safety. Chasing down the Union troopers, one man remembered, "Lomax and the men of the bloody Eleventh were among them, slashing left and right."

Diverging from the artillerists, Lomax then attacked Wyndam's brigade near the railroad. Lomax remembered, "I charged, and drove them from the station." Advancing toward Culpeper, Lomax sent a detachment toward the village and then toward Stevensburg before finally rejoining Stuart.

A company of the 10th New York also lingered behind because the order to withdraw never reached them. A Confederate charge finally chased them off. Fortunately, they escaped without sustaining any casualties.

From his headquarters on Fleetwood Hill, Stuart

watched as Gregg withdrew. With desperate fighting, Stuart parried a major threat to the rear of his line. "Thus ended the attack of Gregg's division upon the Fleetwood Hill," Major McClellan noted. "Modern warfare cannot furnish an instance of a field more closely, more valiantly contested. General Gregg retired from the field defeated, but defiant and unwilling to acknowledge a defeat."

After two hours of ferocious hand-to-hand fighting, Gregg reformed his command in the fields to the south of Brandy Station. Unsupported, Gregg wrote later, "I ordered the withdrawal of my brigades. In good order they left the field, the enemy choosing not to follow."

At Fleetwood Hill

The U.D.C. monument is the only historical monument on the battlefield. (cm)

You are now standing atop Fleetwood Hill. This is the epicenter of the Brandy Station battlefield. Immediately to your left is where Jeb Stuart's headquarters was located. The United Daughters of the Confederacy monument was erected in 1926 to mark the spot and commemorate the battle on property eventually acquired by the Civil War Trust in 2014, which installed the trail and the interpretive markers. If you wish to walk the short loop, keep to your right to follow the action chronologically.

At the crest of the ridge to your right is the area where Major McClellan spotted Gregg's division riding into Brandy Station, which is across Route 15/29 and directly behind you. It was here that Lieutenant Tucker engaged the Federals. Fortuitously, the 12th Virginia Cavalry arrived at the crest as Carter expended his last rounds. By then, the Yankees had nearly reached them.

Here, the Virginians engaged the leading Union regiment, the veteran 1st New Jersey Cavalry. Major Hugh Janeway of the 1st New Jersey remembered that his troopers "rode up the gentle ascent that led to Stuart's headquarters, the men gripping hard their sabers, and the horses taking ravines and ditches in their stride." The Jerseymen briefly gained the crest but were swept away by the attacking Confederates moments later. A Rebel artillerist recalled, "The two

forces met with a crash that could have been heard miles away . . . back and forth they swayed across the slope of Fleetwood Hill." Remembered Maj. Myron Beaumont of the 1st New Jersey:

With the help of Civil War Trails and under the direction of historian Clark "Bud" Hall, the Civil War Trust has interpreted the crest of Fleetwood Hill. (dd)

> *The enemy had withdrawn behind the crest of the hill, and it was not until we were within a hundred yards of the top that they advanced to meet us. They were armed, principally, with pistols and carbines, our men using generally the saber. Then began the most spirited and hardest fought cavalry fight ever known in this country.*

The 1st Pennsylvania Cavalry also joined the contest. A Pennsylvania officer wrote afterwards,

> *Scarcely half the regiment had gotten into position, when the enemy opened a battery . . . from the eminence of the Barbour house . . . when we moved forward it was to storm the position . . . as we marched straight toward the smoking cannons' mounts, they first saluted us with spherical case, and as the distance grew less, hurled grape and canister into our faces.*

As you follow the trail, the Barbour house, also known as Beauregard, is the large brick house across the field on the ridge to your right. Late in the battle, Gen. Robert E. Lee came forward from his camps around Culpeper and observed the closing phases from the front porch of Beauregard. The pond at the base of the ridge was not there in 1863.

Wade Hampton and Judson Kilpatrick started a fued on this field at Brandy Station that would last all the way to Bennett Place, N.C., in April of 1865. (cm)

Arriving to reinforce their fellow Virginians was the hard-fighting 6th Virginia. The engagement continued to sway over the hillside. This combat was so desperate and confusing that one man from the 12th Virginia remembered that he was captured—and escaped—twice as his regiment engaged the Northerners. The 1st New Jersey lost 56 of the 280 men through the course of the three-hour contest.

In the area of tour stop 6, at the base of Fleetwood Hill, Captain Martin deployed a section of his guns. The 6th Virginia made the first attempt to capture them. Lieutenant Robert O. Allen, who had killed Grimes Davis earlier that morning, was severely wounded in the shoulder in this assault. After the repulse of the 6th Virginia, Lt. Col. Elijah White's 35th Battalion of Virginia Cavalry attacked Martin's guns on an axis that followed the route of Fleetwood Heights Road. Martin remembered that "of the 36 men that I took into the engagement, but 6 came out safely, and of these 30, 21 are either killed, wounded, or missing, and scarcely one of them will but carry the honorable mark of the saber or bullet to his grave."

As you pass the gazebo, the area between it and the modern highway is where Hampton's brigade engaged the 2nd and 10th New York from Col. Judson Kilpatrick's brigade. Hampton personally led the assault against the 10th New York. Colonel Pierce

Looking southward from Fleetwood's hilltop. (cm)

M. B. Young, who commanded the Cobb Legion of Hampton's brigade, remembered that his men "swept the hill clear of the enemy, he being scattered and entirely routed." Young's men received the personal compliments of Jeb Stuart, who rode up to them and declared, "Cobb's Legion, you've covered yourselves with glory."

Later in the action, the 1st Maine Cavalry charged directly toward where you are standing and across the face of Fleetwood Hill. Finally reaching the vicinity of Beauregard, the unsupported regiment was forced to ride through the fighting to reach the safety of the Union lines.

But Flew the Sabres

CHAPTER NINE

As Stuart and Gregg desperately contested possession of Fleetwood Hill, and tethered by Alfred Pleasonton's passivity, Brig. Gen. John Buford remained stuck in his position opposite the now-abandoned Confederate line at St. James Church. Rooney Lee's brigade were the only remaining Confederates in Buford's immediate front. These men continued harassing Buford from behind the stone wall.

In response, a squadron of the 2nd U.S. and the 8th Illinois attacked the wall in an attempt to drive off Lee's sharpshooters. The Confederates turned them back. An Illinois sergeant recalled the Confederates' "fire too severe to admit of his turning their flank as easily as had been imagined."

A concerted attack would have overwhelmed Lee's line by a sheer force of numbers and would have allowed Buford to turn the enemy line and envelop Stuart. Pleasonton, however, was still operating under a cloud of caution and would not authorize a full-scale attack.

Buford instead resolved to outflank Lee's position.

Approaching Capt. George Stevenson of the 3rd Wisconsin Infantry and Capt. Daniel Oakey of the 2nd Massachusetts Infantry, Buford asked, "Do you see those people down there? They've got to be driven out." Stevenson replied, "It's about double our force," prompting Oakey to add, "Fully that, if not more." Buford responded, "Well, I didn't order you, mind: but, if you think you can flank them, go in, and drive them off."

Wesley Merritt's Federal cavalry moved across Yew Ridge from left to right to strike Rooney Lee's horsemen. (cm)

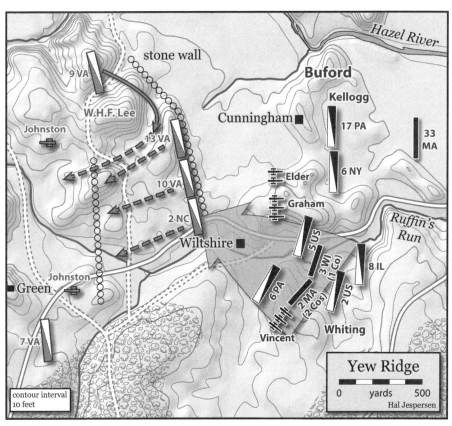

YEW RIDGE—For the better part of the day, Brig. Gen. W.H.F "Rooney" Lee's troopers had stymied Buford on the Cunningham Farm, just north of St. James Church. Lee's men had utilized a stone wall from which he had repulsed several Union assaults. After several hours, Buford finally pried Lee from the position. Lee was wounded shortly thereafter during a melee.

Oakey later wrote, "It would hardly do to back out in the presence of so distinguished a cavalry audience, if there was a chance of success." Buford's presence with the infantry quickly drew a volley from the stone wall. The old dragoon ignored their requests to move to a safer vantage point.

Hidden from Confederate view by woods and the surrounding terrain, Stevenson and Oakey sent several companies of infantry unseen through cornfields and behind hedges until they reached a point from which they could enfilade the enemy line. The Northern officers then ordered 10 sharpshooters forward into a wheat field while the rest of the infantrymen deployed as skirmishers. Reaching their position, the marksmen opened fire on Lee's flank, shocking the unsuspecting

Confederates. After the war, the regimental historian of the 3rd Wisconsin remembered that "some crawled off on their hands and knees; others fell dead or writhed in wounds; and a number surrendered. . . . The killed, wounded, and captured outnumbered the force that executed this movement."

Inspired by the infantry attack, Buford directed Maj. Henry C. Whelan, now commanding the 6th Pennsylvania, to charge the position. Supported by Capt. Wesley Merritt's 2nd U.S., the Pennsylvanians bore down on the 10th Virginia. Major Whelan had his horse

Wesley Merritt vs. Rooney Lee— and out flew the sabres! (loc)

Lancer shot out from under him during the attack and later called the stone wall "decidedly the hottest place I was ever in. A man could not show his head or a finger without a hundred rifle shots whistling about. The air [was] almost solid with lead."

The fighting quickly escalated. Led by the brave charge of the Pennsylvanians, the Yankees moved forward until they met with a stiff counterattack.

With sabers drawn, the 9th Virginia slammed into the charging Keystoners. The Pennsylvanians reeled in "confusion . . . directly on the stone fence through which there was but a narrow opening; and dealing them some heavy blows during the necessary delay in forcing their way through it. They were followed by men of the Ninth at a gallop through the field beyond the fence to the edge of the woods, where a Federal battery was in position. A good many of the prisoners which the Federals had taken were released by this charge."

Elements of the 6th U.S. commanded by Capt. Henry McQuiston and James Brisbin received orders to extend the Union line so as to overlap the end of the Confederate line. Spotting a large battle flag on Yew Ridge, the two squadrons of the 6th U.S. rode right for it. Major Charles Whiting, who commanded the Reserve Brigade, recalled that his

A protégé of John Buford's, Capt. Wesley Merritt received a promotion to brigadier general at the end of June and served with the Cavalry Corps through the remainder of the war. In the postwar years, Merritt commanded the 9th U.S. and 5th U.S. Cavalry and led American forces in the Philippines during the Spanish-American War. (loc)

men twice charged the enemy, "each time driving him with severe loss . . . to a hill beyond and holding him in check against heavy odds."

Captain McQuiston remembered, "With many cheers our men left their position, rushed forward across the open field, firing as they moved on . . . all were repulsed . . . and returned to the position they had left." The pressure became too much for Rooney Lee's men, who eventually withdrew behind Yew Ridge.

Interestingly, some 200 feet from the Confederate line was a ditch partially filled with water. Crossing it, the Regulars saw several of their comrades, probably from the 6th Pennsylvania, rise from it. "In one of the earlier charges of the morning these men had reached this ditch . . . and afraid to return under fire of rebel bullets had sought safety," one said. "[H]ere they had lain since morning . . . under the broiling sun. The poor fellows must have been greatly relieved when we passed over them."

Receiving orders to attack, McQuiston and Brisbin moved out. Riding up Yew Ridge, they emerged on the crest. McQuiston wrote, "a troop of cavalry with gray horses was rushing rapidly up the steep slope, while the rebels were disappearing down the slope on the opposite side . . . this troop of ours disappeared from view . . . but it did not remain away long, being driven in turn by greater numbers. Meanwhile my troop and that of Capt. Brisbin followed the retreating enemy."

Lieutenant Isaac Ward moved his squadron to the rear of the 9th Virginia Cavalry. As the Virginians moved past his position, Ward charged. "It was a curious scene," remembered Pvt. Sidney Davis, "this small body so boldly attacking a large force that was at this moment driving from their front quite a strong regiment [the 6th Pennsylvania Cavalry], but the movement was successful." Although he was mortally wounded while attempting to seize an enemy battle flag, Ward saved the Pennsylvanians.

The Yankees fell back, closely pursued on foot by their foes. One officer in blue on the right of the 6th U.S. dismounted his troopers and "managed in this way, by stopping every minute and fighting the rebels, in getting my men safely out of the wood. The ground sloped downward for 30 or 40 yards and then raised again, just beyond to a little knoll . . . I saw at once that the rebels would have every chance of murdering us, as we crossed this low ground, exposed completely to their fire from behind trees." The Regulars returned the volleys. "The next minute," the officer recalled, "I had gained the knoll with my squadron, and just behind it, I ordered them to stop, and give it to the rebels." The Confederates then retreated "in great haste."

The 2nd U.S. entered the seesaw fight and came to the aid of the 6th Pennsylvania and 6th U.S. "At last an order—which we all had hoped and all but asked for, and which General Buford told me he was anxious to give, but had not the authority, but which no doubt he carried—finally came," recalled the commander of the 2nd U.S., Capt. Wesley Merritt. "We were ordered to advance and deal on their ground with the batteries and sharpshooters which had wrought such havoc among our men and horses."

Supported by horse artillery fire, Merritt's troopers slammed into the flank of the 9th Virginia, driving the Rebels back onto the northern extension of Fleetwood Hill. "Out flew the sabres, and most handsomely they were used," Buford wrote.

"We rode . . . with sabers in hand at the astonished enemy," Merritt added. "The next moment [the Rebel line] had broken and was flying, while horsemen of the Second mingling with the enemy, dealt saber blows and pistol shots . . . friend and foe, mixed inextricably together, rode on in this terrible carnage, each apparently for the same destination."

Merritt's determined charge carried the regiment up and onto Yew Ridge and "in its impetuosity, carried everything before it. It bore up the hill, across the plateau, and to the crest on the other side." On the far side, they saw a startling sight. "There were discovered in the valley below, fresh regiments of horse moving quietly towards the scene of our combat anxious to strike us while we were in confusion," Merritt wrote.

The assault of the 2nd U.S. threated Lee's brigade. Lee, in turn, decided to order his three uncommitted regiments—the 2nd North Carolina, the 10th Virginia, and the 13th Virginia—into the fight. They

The second son of Robert E. Lee, "Rooney" Lee attended Harvard prior to the war. He led the 9th Virginia Cavalry throughout the campaigns of 1862. (usahec)

drew sabers and advanced to meet Merritt. William Royall of the 9th Virginia remembered that

> *about 4 o'clock in the afternoon Lee put himself at the head of my regiment . . . and gave the order to charge up the hill, he riding at the head . . . when we got to the summit of the hill, there, some two hundred yards away, stood a long line of blue-coated cavalry. Lee . . . dashed at the center of this line with his column of fours. The Yankees were . . . cut in two . . . but each of their flanks closed in . . . and then a most terrible affray with sabers and pistols took place. We got the best of it, and we had soon killed, wounded, or captured almost all of them.*

Colonel Solomon Williams, commander of the 2nd North Carolina, and a member of the West Point Class of 1858, received permission to enter the fight. This was Williams' first time in combat, and he formed his regiment by squadron and advanced at a gallop. The 10th Virginia advanced with the North Carolinians. The Virginians stopped and opened fire while the Tar Heels drew sabers and charged. Captain William Graham of the 2nd North Carolina recalled, "the regiment raised the yell as it went by our stationary and retiring companions . . . the Federals were the fleers and the Confederates the pursuers. Our regiment drove the enemy about half a mile back."

Colonel Williams himself led the charge. When the man next to him was shot down, he yelled, "Second North Carolina, follow me." Captain Graham cried out, "Colonel, we had better get a line, they are too strong to take this way." Williams replied, "That will be best: where is the flag?" Turning to ride back to the flag, Williams was shot and killed. He was married just two weeks earlier, and his brother-in-law later took his body home for burial. Williams' fall broke up the charge of the Carolinians.

Major Joseph T. Rosser led the charge of the 10th Virginia. Rosser spotted a lone Federal officer in front of the line, drew his saber, and engaged the officer, prompting Pvt. John Smith of Co. F of the 10th Virginia to call out, "Hurray for Hell, Wade in!"

The charge by the 2nd North Carolina and the 10th Virginia shoved the Regulars back.

As his men retreated, Merritt and his aide, Lt. James Quirk, found themselves surrounded by the Confederates. Still believing that his regiment was with him, Merritt carried only his courage and saber. A group of Confederate officers spotted him, and one yelled, "Kill the damned Yankee!" Rather than ride for safety, Merritt boldly approached the man he thought was their leader, brought his saber to a point, and demanded, "Colonel, you are my prisoner!" The officer he had approached was not a colonel, but Rooney Lee himself. "The hell I am!" Lee shouted and swung his saber. Merritt parried the blow, but Lee's saber pierced Merritt's hat and a kerchief that he had tied around his head as a sweatband, nicking his scalp. Merritt and Quirk fled when the Rebel officers opened fire. Amidst a hail of pistol shots and echoing cries of his surrender, Merritt safely reached his own lines, where, "a kindly Hibernian gave me the hat off his own head."

Seeing the Federals retreat, Rooney Lee gave the command, "'Forward,' and was at the same instant wounded," Lt. George Beale of the 9th Virginia wrote. "General Lee directed in person the countercharge, and as his mounted men swept over the hill . . . a bullet passed through his leg, in the moment of victory." Their commander out of action, the brigade broke off the fight to join Stuart on Fleetwood Hill.

Meanwhile, Fitz Lee's brigade, led by Col. Thomas T. Munford, arrived on Yew Ridge as the battle

From Buford's Knoll, Yew Ridge is visible in the far distance. Part of the stone wall runs through the treeline on the left and then takes a right-angle turn through the far treeline. (dd)

dissipated. When the day began, Munford's men were guarding the Hazel River, a tributary of the Rappahannock. With vague orders in hand, three of his regiments, the 1st, 2nd, and 3rd Virginia, crossed the river at Starke's Ford, and advanced to the Rappahannock. Munford arrived there about 11 a.m., only to find the Federals present in force. Munford then detoured and headed to Beverly's Ford, only to turn around and then march to Welford's Ford.

Arriving there about 4 p.m. and in full view of the fighting on Yew Ridge, Munford deployed a skirmish line supported by Capt. James Breathed's battery of horse artillery. "The enemy's right flank being protected . . . " Munford remembered, "made it impracticable at any time to engage them in a hand-to-hand fight." Nonetheless, as one of Breathed's officers recalled, "We had it all our own way."

Munford maintained his position until Buford broke off contact and withdrew. Writing later, Munford stated he could see "a division of cavalry, a brigade of infantry, and two or three detachments of dismounted cavalry." The Confederates followed but found themselves unable to engage.

Thomas L. Rosser, a fellow cavalryman who greatly disliked Munford, stated in a speech after the war, "On the other flank the unfortunate absence of our gallant and wide-awake Fitz Lee from his brigade (he being absent sick), left his splendid regiments and Breathed's battery in less able hands, which, in consequence . . . did not reach the battlefield until very late in the day." However, the addition of these veterans may very well have made a difference in the fighting.

After the battle, Buford wrote that his men "gained the crest overlooking Brandy Station," but that they could not hold it. "The enemy, although vastly superior in numbers was fought hand to hand and . . . not allowed to gain an inch of ground."

After 14 long hours of fighting, Buford slowly and defiantly withdrew back across the Rappahannock.

With a coordinated effort on the part of Pleasonton, Buford and Gregg may very well have joined forces and captured Yew Ridge and Fleetwood Hill. The Federal cavalry chief, however, remained content to hold his position. The added weight of Duffié's command would also have been helpful. Duffié,

"THE ENEMY, ALTHOUGH VASTLY SUPERIOR IN NUMBERS, WAS FOUGHT HAND TO HAND AND . . . NOT ALLOWED TO GAIN AN INCH OF GROUND."

— *John Buford*

however, became engaged elsewhere and did not arrive in time to make a difference.

➤ TO STOP 8

Cautiously turn around at the lower end of the parking lot and take a left onto Fleetwood Heights Road. Proceed down the valley to your first stop sign. Turn left and proceed through the traffic light across Route 15/29 toward Brandy Station. At the first stop sign, turn left onto Carrico Mills Road (Route 669) and proceed 5.6 miles to the intersection of Carrico Mills Road and Germanna Highway (Route 3). Turn right onto Route 3. You are now following the advance of Duffié's division as they approached Stevensburg.

In 1.4 miles you will reach the intersection of Route 3 and Clay Hill Road. Cautiously pull over. The high ground to your front is Hansborough Ridge.

GPS: 38° 27.352′ N, 77° 54.027′ W

Willis Madden built and operated a tavern out of this building, LaGrange, situated just south of Brandy Station on Stevensburg Road. Madden, a free black, lived in the structure with his family. He also constructed a blacksmith shop and store to assist in the needs of the travelers. Modern travelers will see it on the way to Stop 8. (cm)(cm)

The Fight at Stevensburg

CHAPTER TEN

Following their crossing of Kelly's Ford, Second Division commander Col. Alfred N. Duffié, operating under the orders of Brig. Gen. David Gregg, was instructed to move "directly upon Stevensburg, following the road leading to Raccoon Ford." Upon his arrival, Duffié was to "halt and communicate with our forces at Brandy Station, and from this point communication will be had with you . . . [I]t is intended that when the right of our line at Brandy Station advances toward Culpeper, your division at Stevensburg will also move upon Culpeper."

Colonel Luigi Palma di Cesnola's brigade led Duffié's advance. Colenel di Cesnola placed the 1st Massachusetts on the left, and the 1st Rhode Island and 6th Ohio on the right. The 3rd Pennsylvania made up the brigade's reserve. Duffié then commenced the march to Stevensburg.

To feel out what was in front of him, Duffié deployed a battalion of the 6th Ohio under Maj. Benhamin C. Stanhope ahead of the column. "The first squadron found the enemy in some force in the town," an Ohio officer recalled, "but drove them out at a run." The Ohioans in turn "were compelled to retire in turn before two regiments of the enemy, who advanced upon them. Slowly retiring . . . they held the enemy in check until the main body came up."

Around 8:30, Major Stanhope reported that he had reached Stevensburg. In the rear of the column, Lt. William Brooke-Rawle of the 3rd Pennsylvania

A monument to Will Farley occupies the knoll in the vicinity of where he was wounded. (cm)

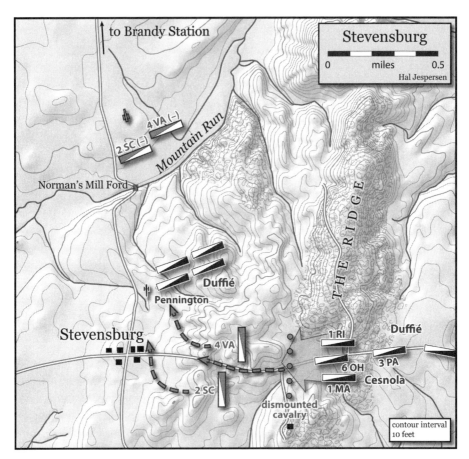

Stevensburg—While the fighting raged at Brandy Station, Col. Alfred Duffié's Union troopers advanced to the south toward Stevensburg. The Federals encountered Confederate cavalry east of the village. After a sharp fight, the Rebels withdrew to a new position above Mountain Run. Before Duffié could launch an assault, he received instructions to disengage and reinforce the Federals engaged at Brandy Station.

Cavalry rode to an eminence to observe the brigade's movement. "I caught a beautiful glimpse of the advance . . ." he later wrote. "The skirmishers deployed in front, supported by their reserves . . . with the artillery, advancing on our left along the road, & our regiment advancing in echelons of squadrons supporting both the battery & skirmishers."

Earlier that morning, Brig. Gen. Wade Hampton's foresight ensured that the Confederate left would be guarded. Learning of the Union crossing at Kelly's Ford, Hampton ordered Col. Matthew C. Butler's 2nd South Carolina Cavalry to Brandy Station. Before breaking camp, Butler dispatched Capt. Leonard Williams' squadron to Stevensburg. Not long after

their arrival, Williams spotted the head of Duffié's command. "When a regiment and then a brigade of Yankees came in sight and drew up in battle line, I attracted their attention," he remembered. The Yankees "threw out their skirmishers the length of a mile in front of me. They advanced briskly. I kept out my videttes . . . hold them in check as long as possible." After deploying his troopers, Williams sent a courier to Butler to inform him of this development. Butler immediately turned his regiment and marched to Stevensburg.

Screening the countryside between Stevensburg and Culpeper was of the utmost importance to the Confederates. Lieutenant General James Longstreet's First Corps was camped nearby at Pony Mountain. If Duffié discovered the presence of the infantry, it would seriously threaten Lee's invasion plans. Recognizing the gravity of the moment, Butler sent his second-in-command, Lt. Col. Frank Hampton, the younger brother of Wade Hampton, ahead toward Stevensburg. Hampton was directed to do whatever he could do to slow the enemy advance. At the same time, Butler ordered Maj. Thomas J. Lipscomb eastward toward Hansbrough's Ridge and another 40 troopers to swing east toward Cole's Hill and then to turn south toward Stevensburg to intercept Stanhope.

Butler hoped that Hampton would take up a position on Hansborough's Ridge, east of Stevensburg. While his regiment only numbered around 200 men,

Alexander Pennington deployed two of his guns at the top of this knoll. (dd)

Heavily engaged at Fleetwood Hill, Wade Hampton was unable to reach his brother, Frank (above), before the younger Hampton died of wounds received at Stevensburg. (usc)

Will Farley's death deprived the Confederate cavalry of one of its most skilled scouts. (vhs)

deploying on the ridge would give them the advantage of high ground.

Arriving in Stevensburg, Hampton found that some of the Federals had already passed through but then withdrew when they encountered Rebel skirmishers. Reaching the grounds of Salubria, a nearby plantation house, Hampton chose to dismount part of his contingent while keeping the rest of his men mounted. The dismounted troopers deployed directly in front of the house.

As their Northern counterparts approached, the South Carolinians unleashed a volley. One Union officer remembered that the well-protected Confederates "fired upon our men, who were mounted, and made the advance uncomfortable. . . . No carbine in the hands of a dismounted man under cover is certainly worth half a dozen hands of men on horseback; and these men of Hampton . . . delivered a hot fire upon the advance of the 1st Massachusetts, which was opposed to them." Hampton then ordered his force of 36 men to charge. A Pennsylvanian recalled that they "charged the First Massachusetts Cavalry down a hollow road." The badly outnumbered Rebels were quickly repulsed. Their brief action, however, bought precious time for Butler to reach Stevensburg with the rest of his command.

As Butler deployed his troopers, the famous Confederate scout, Capt. Will Farley, rode up with a welcome message. Stuart, upon learning of the threat, had sent a piece of artillery, along with Col. Williams C. Wickham's 4th Virginia Cavalry, to assist Butler. As the 4th Virginia—the famous Black Horse Cavalry—approached the field, Wickham sent Lt. Col. William H. Payne forward to find Butler, who "requested Colonel Payne to inform Colonel Wickham of the disposition I had made of the few men at my disposal and to say to him . . . I would cheerfully take orders from him." The South Carolinian was junior in rank to Wickham, who declined to assume command. Accordingly, Butler asked Wickham to send two mounted squadrons to reinforce Hampton, while the rest of the regiment deployed alongside the 2nd South Carolina.

Surprised by the sudden charge of Hampton's men, Duffié turned his attention to this enemy contingent. He recalled, "I immediately threw forward the skirmishers of the First Massachusetts, First Rhode Island and Sixth Ohio Cavalry, who . . . became engaged with the enemy, who were strongly posted and partly concealed in the woods." Throwing his troopers at the Rebels, Duffié scattered the Confederates. "We charged," wrote a member of the 1st Massachusetts. "They mounted their horses in a hurry and skedaddled."

Butler recalled the moment. "Imagine my surprise when I learned . . . that a regiment of the enemy's cavalry had charged Colonel Hampton's handful of men and swept him out of the road." In the ensuing fight, "Colonel Hampton received a pistol ball in the pit of his stomach and died that afternoon from the effects of it."

The Union assault smashed into Butler's line, cutting the Virginia squadrons sent to reinforce Hampton in two. "No sooner did our sabers appear gleaming in front than a panic seemed to seize the whole mass," remembered an officer of the 6th Ohio Cavalry. A soldier in the 4th Virginia remembered that the regiment "ran like sheep and had all the fight taken out of them that day." Wickham himself fled with the 1st Massachusetts in hot pursuit. Much of the regiment withdrew as far as Pony Mountain, effectively taking them out of the battle. Wickham, however, took full responsibility for retreat: "I regard the conduct of my regiment, in which I have heretofore had perfect confidence, as so disgraceful in this instance."

Following the charge, Duffié reformed his regiments and resumed the advance. He deployed Lt. Alexander C. M. Pennington's Battery M, 2nd U.S. Artillery, on a knoll overlooking Mountain Run. After Pennington's batteries opened, Duffié ordered his men forward.

As the Federals approached, a defiant Will Farley drew his revolver, rode forward, and began firing. "I gave the command, 'Commence firing' all along the line," recounted Butler. "I noticed a mounted cavalryman in blue slide off his horse . . . very easily, and the horse trot back to his rear, and assumed he had dismounted not more than fifty yards down the hill for the purpose of getting the protection of a tree in his future efforts."

This action was intended to delay the Yankees

A South Carolinian, Matthew Butler was a lawyer prior to enlisting in the Hampton Legion. He fought at First Manassas and was promoted to Colonel of the 2nd South Carolina Cavalry in August 1862. (usc)

A talented artillerist, A. C. M. Pennington would go on to render invaluable service at Gettysburg. His skills did not go unnoticed by his superiors, and he steadily rose through the ranks to command a brigade by war's end. (loc)

Born in Paris, France, Alfred Duffié, was educated at the military college of St. Cyr and saw action in the Crimea. He emigrated to the U.S. in 1859 and served in the 2nd New York and 1st Rhode Island Cavalry early in the conflict. (loc)

because the collapse of the 4th Virginia had turned the Confederate flank, forcing Butler to withdraw to a low ridge on the north bank of Mountain Run near Norman's Mill, above Stevensburg. Sending his adjutant back to Stuart to inform him he had abandoned Stevensburg, Butler reformed his men and his lone piece of artillery at his new position. The gun opened counterbattery fire with Pennington's guns, thereby distracting the Union horse artillery from firing on the Confederate troopers. This artillery fire proved detrimental to the 2nd South Carolina. As Butler conversed with Farley, a Union shell struck and then ricocheted some 30 feet away. It careened toward the two men, striking them both. Farley suffered a mortal wound, and Butler lost a leg. Command of the regiment fell to Major Lipscomb. Although badly wounded, Butler ordered Lipscomb to "continue to fight and fall back slowly toward Culpeper."

Meanwhile, Duffié prepared the 1st Massachusetts to charge Lipscomb's position. However, orders from Gregg arrived before the Frenchman could execute his attack. "Return and join the Third Division, on the road to Brandy Station," instructed Gregg.

From his vantage point overlooking Mountain Run, Duffié could see the battle several miles away on Fleetwood Hill. Complying with the directive, Duffié disengaged. He easily could have broken through Lipscomb's thin line but instead chose to take a longer route to Fleetwood Hill, assuring that he would arrive too late to support Gregg's attack. He left behind part of the 3rd Pennsylvania to watch the 2nd South Carolina.

Following suit, Lipscomb also withdrew to a position closer to Culpeper, where he eventually made contact with Wickham. In turn, Wickham ordered Lipscomb to return to his position and to follow Duffié. Reaching Stevensburg once again, Lipscomb found that the 3rd Pennsylvania had already departed, allowing him to follow Duffié unmolested.

Hearing the heavy firing on Fleetwood Hill, the Pennsylvanians rode toward Brandy Station, arriving just as the battle ended. One of the Keystoners remembered, "After remaining for about an hour . . . we withdrew to Rappahannock Station and crossed the Ford, having moved along the road which our troops had gained." Covering the withdrawal of Duffié's division, they eventually exchanged long-range fire with Lipscomb's troopers.

While Lipscomb headed back to Stevensburg, Duffié rode toward Brandy Station, eventually encountering a routed squadron of the 10th New York. Believing that Confederate cavalry was nearby, Duffié spent half an hour deploying into line of battle. When no enemy force materialized, he continued onward and linked up with Gregg. As the blue horsemen withdrew from the battlefield, Duffié deployed his guns to cover the withdrawal.

Unfortunately for Gregg, as well as Alfred Pleasonton, Duffié and his veteran division did not participate in the great cavalry fight at Fleetwood Hill. "We were driven about in a circle all day seeking Pleasonton and finding Rebel batteries," steamed Col. William Doster of the 4th Pennsylvania.

Duffié had obeyed Pleasonton's orders about guarding the Federal flank. However, Pleasonton's flawed plan meant that by foraying to Stevensburg, Duffié missed out on the main battle. Butler's intrepid band had fought well by keeping 1,900 enemy troopers occupied who may very well have made a difference at Brandy Station.

As far as the fight at Stevensburg was concerned, Duffié only committed three regiments—half of his available force—to combat. His entire force may very well have broken through Butler's line before he reformed along Mountain Run, thereby opening a direct route to Fleetwood Hill for Duffié, which would have provided Gregg with another division to utilize. These additional numbers could very well have tipped

An artillery piece still stands today near Butler's position. (dd)

the balance in the fighting for Fleetwood Hill.

Duffié's troopers were frustrated by the fact that they did not see more action. A sergeant in the 16th Pennsylvania wrote, "Am just too sorry that I and our squad could not perform our part in this day's fighting."

Toward Mountain Run

A historical marker stands at the entrance to Salubria. (cm)

As you continue on Route 3 another 0.6 miles past Hansborough Ridge, you will see a historical marker for Salubria and a driveway leading back to the house. This is where Lt. Col. Frank Hampton first engaged Duffié's column. After repulsing the foray, Duffié remembered that as his men moved forward:

The enemy were quickly dislodged from those dense woods into open fields, where the First Rhode Island Cavalry was ordered to charge on the right, the First Massachusetts on the left, and one squadron of the Sixth Ohio Cavalry on the road, in order to cut off the retreat of the enemy on his flank and check him in his front.

In this area, Frank Hampton was shot while exchanging saber slashes with a Yankee trooper. Then engaged with Gregg atop Fleetwood Hill, Wade Hampton did not reach his mortally wounded brother's side until it was too late. Frank Hampton died at Salubria.

Built in the late 1750s, Salubria is now administered by the Germanna Foundation. The house does not have regular hours; however, tours are available from the foundation by appointment from April to October.

After the war, Wade Hampton blamed Williams Wickham for his brother's death. If not for "he fact that the Fourth Virginia Cavalry, under the command of Colonel Wickham, broke and ran . . ." he bitterly wrote, "my brother, Lieutenant Colonel Frank Hampton, would not have been killed that day."

As you pass the Salubria marker, notice to your immediate right front the Stevensburg Baptist Church. Continue 0.7 miles after passing Salubria, and turn right onto the Stevensburg Road. Then, in 0.1 mile, make a right onto York Road. Follow York Road to the entrance to the church. Please remain in your vehicle and be respectful, as this is an active congregation. Pass behind the church to your left and you will see a modern house on a knoll to your left. This knoll is where Lt. Alexander C. M. Pennington deployed Battery M, 2nd U.S. Artillery; from here, he fired the artillery shot that killed Will Farley and took off Matthew C. Butler's leg. Circle through the parking lot and return to the Stevensburg Road.

Turn right and proceed 0.8 miles. After you cross Mountain Run, turn right into the parking lot near the monument and interpretive signs. Park and get out of your car.

GPS: 38° 27.352′N, 77° 54.027′W

This sign marks the entrance to Stevensburg Baptist Church. (cm)

At Mountain Run: Butler's Position

Below you on the road was Norman's Mill Ford. Quite narrow, it was the only place along Mountain Run where horses could cross. You are now standing in the area where Butler redeployed after withdrawing from Stevensburg. The lone gun sent by Stuart was positioned nearby.

As the artillery engaged Pennington, Farley and Butler sat on their horses facing opposite directions. The two chuckled while Butler, who was known for his courage under fire, shared with Farley a story about a Yankee officer killed by his own men. Butler had his back to Pennington's position, when, he remembered,

[a] twelve pound shell from the enemy's gun on the hill (we had evidently been located by

a field glass), struck the ground about thirty steps from our position in an open field ricocheted and passed through my right leg above the ankle, through Farley's horse, and took off his right leg at the knee. My horse bounded in the air, threw me, saddle and all, flat on my back in the road, when the poor fellow moved off with his entrails hanging out towards the clover field where he had been grazing in the early morning and died there, as I was afterwards informed.

Farley's mortally wounded horse fell in the road.

"As soon as we discovered what the trouble was," Butler continued, "my first apprehension was we would bleed to death before assistance could reach us. I therefore directed Farley to get out his handkerchief and make a tourniquet by binding around his leg above the wound." Butler was able to tie a tourniquet until his regimental surgeon arrived to amputate his shattered leg. As Farley was carried from the field, he asked that his leg be brought to him, remarking, "It is an old friend, gentlemen, and I do not wish to part from it."

Mountain Run provided a natural barrier to Butler's position after the withdrawal from Stevensburg. (dd)

Butler "was placed on a blanket," he remembered afterwards, "and with a man at each corner . . . they walked with every possible care. The grating of the bones was anything but pleasant." Taken to a grove of trees nearby, Butler's men assembled a stretcher.

Farley died as the result of his wounds. Butler, however, had his leg amputated and survived. Returning to the field, he distinguished himself a year later at the battle of Trevilian Station, in the operations around Petersburg and in the Carolinas campaign. After the war, Butler was elected to the United States Senate from South Carolina. When war with Spain broke out in 1898, Butler accepted a commission as Major General of United States Volunteers. He passed away on April 14, 1909, and was buried in Edgefield, South Carolina.

⟶ TO STOP 1

Turn right out of the parking lot. In 0.4 miles, you will see two houses on the right, back to back. The small yellow house in the rear is where Matthew Butler was taken following his wounding, and where his leg was amputated. This house is private property, so please respect the owners' rights.

Continue for 2.5 miles to the stop sign. Turn left onto Carrico Mill Road and then turn right onto Brandy Road 0.1 mile later.

In another 0.1 mile, turn right into the parking lot of the Graffiti House. You may remain here for the final chapters of the narrative.

A Reluctant Withdrawal

CHAPTER ELEVEN

Earlier in the day, Brig. Gen. Alfred Pleasonton received permission from Maj. Gen. Joseph Hooker to withdraw from the field at his discretion. As evening approached, Gregg's division had already disengaged from Fleetwood Hill and was heading back to Kelly's Ford, where it would re-cross the Rappahannock River. Pleasonton decided that his men had done all they could for one day and ordered John Buford to pull his men back across the Rappahannock. The staff officer sent by Pleasonton found the Kentuckian "entirely isolated from the rest of the command under Pleasonton . . . but paying no attention and fighting straight on."

Buford wrote later that as the firing waned on Fleetwood Hill, "I was ordered to withdraw. Abundance of means was sent to aid me, and we came off the field in fine shape and at our convenience. Capt. [Richard S.C.] Lord with the 1st U.S. came up fresh comparatively with plenty of ammunition and entirely relieved my much exhausted but undaunted command in a most commendable style. The engagement lasted near 14 hours."

With the 1st U.S. and the added protection of Brig. Gen. Adelbert Ames' infantry covering their withdrawal, Buford's men leisurely splashed their way across Beverly Ford to the Fauquier County side. Defiantly, Buford himself "came along serenely at a moderate walk." The 33rd Massachusetts Infantry served as a rear guard. When all of the horse soldiers were across to the north bank, the Bay Staters followed.

A peaceful location today, the Cunningham farm saw some of the last action on the field during the battle. (cm)

The Yankee troopers stubbornly left the field and moved through this area toward Beverly Ford. (dd)

The gray-clad cavalry did not hinder the crossing.

Back on the north side of the Rappahannock, Buford joined Pleasonton and a number of staff officers to observe the crossing as the sun set. "Our cavalry fell back across the river that night," wrote one of Buford's unbowed troopers, surprised at the abandonment of the field. "It was a mystery to the boys why they fell back."

Pleasonton, for his part, seemed satisfied. "General Buford withdrew his command in beautiful style to this side," he later wrote, "the enemy not daring to follow, but showing his chagrin and mortification by an angry and sharp cannonading." A reporter traveling with Pleasonton correctly observed, "the fact that the rebels did not take a step toward following the command, though vastly superior in numbers, indicates very clearly that they had had quite enough of the Yankees for one day."

* * *

"I did what you wanted, crippled Stuart so that he can not go on a raid . . ." Pleasonton wrote in a 9:30 p.m. note to Hooker at army headquarters. "My own losses were very heavy, particularly in officers. I never saw greater gallantry . . . exhibited then on the occasion of the fierce 14 hours of fighting from 5 in the morning until 7 at night."

Pleasonton wrote that "Buford's cavalry had a long and desperate encounter, hand to hand, with the enemy, in which he drove handsomely before him very superior forces. Over two hundred prisoners were captured, and one battle flag." Most importantly for the Union cavalry, "the troops are in splendid spirits, and are entitled to the highest praise for their distinguished conduct."

Buford's loss amounted to 36 officers and 435 enlisted men killed, wounded, and missing, for total casualties of 471. This was more than 50 percent of the total Union casualties for the day, which numbered 866. The 6th Pennsylvania Cavalry suffered the worst, losing 108 men, including eight officers. The 2nd U.S. Cavalry lost 66 killed or wounded out of 225 present for duty during the day's fight. Along with these losses, a large number of horses were killed or wounded, leaving many troopers dismounted.

"No regiment engaged that day on the Union side had more of it than ours . . ." remembered a trooper in Grimes Davis' 8th New York. "It was first in and last out in our division. It was not later than 4:30 a.m. in going in, and was rear-guard at the Ford."

But John Buford was rightfully very proud of the performance of all of his troopers. "The men and officers of the entire command without exception behaved with great gallantry," he wrote.

*   *   *

After Duffié's arrival, Gregg had moved to realign his men with Buford's position. The Confederates also shifted, but as Gregg prepared to attack again, he received orders from Pleasonton to withdraw. Brigadier General David Russell's brigade, which had spent the day lightly skirmishing with Brig. Gen. Beverly Robertson's North Carolinians, covered the Pennsylvanian's retreat. "While Pleasonton was defeated at Brandy Station, he made a masterly withdrawal of his forces," a Virginian remembered.

Stuart remembered that Buford's attack on the northern end of Fleetwood Hill "made it absolutely necessary to desist from our pursuit of the force retreating toward Kelly's particularly as the infantry

Matthew Butler was taken to a nearby home, still standing, after he was wounded. (dd)

known to be on that road would very soon have terminated the pursuit."

With that, the largest cavalry fight ever seen in the Western Hemisphere came to an end.

Gregg may have lost the best opportunity for victory that day. He suffered high casualties, including a brigade commander (Wyndham), two regimental commanders, a third field-grade officer wounded, two line officers killed and 15 wounded, 18 enlisted men killed, 65 wounded, and 272 missing. His men captured eight commissioned officers and two sets of colors. Gregg singled out Cols. Percy Wyndham and Judson Kilpatrick for particular praise, and also praised the performance of Capt. Joseph Martin's New York artillerists.

Gregg, however, laid the failure to carry Fleetwood Hill squarely at the feet of Duffié, who had encountered issues with reaching his river crossing and arrived on the battlefield late. Realizing that Stuart's whole force was in front of him, Gregg should have sent for Duffié. He certainly could have used the additional division in a sort of hammer-and-anvil maneuver, with Duffié acting as the hammer driving Stuart's troopers against Gregg's anvil.

At the same time, the cautious Pleasonton, who held Buford in check for several hours, could have released the First Division, freeing further troopers to try to catch Stuart in a trap on Fleetwood Hill.

For all the boldness he expressed in his memo,

Pleasonton's assertion that the Union cavalry had dealt a serious blow to Stuart was false. Brandy Station cost the Confederates 51 killed, 250 wounded, and 132 missing. The Federals suffered 484 killed and wounded and 372 taken prisoner. These losses illustrate the intensity of the fighting—but even though Confederates received several well-placed blows, their cavalry was as formidable as ever.

The opportunity to destroy the Confederate cavalry had slipped through the fingers of the Union command.

*   *   *

Holding the field at the end of the day, Stuart ordered that his headquarters be established once again on Fleetwood Hill, symbolizing his successful defense of the position. While this was a moment of triumph for Stuart, dead and wounded men and horses littered the hill. The flies were "swarming so thick over the blood stains on the ground" that there were very few spots for the Confederates to pitch their tents. Exhausted and hungry, many of the Southern troopers simply collapsed where they stood.

Stuart remembered the fight for Fleetwood Hill as "long and spirited." He generally praised all of his brigade commanders, but especially praising Brig. Gens. Grumble Jones and Wade Hampton while severely criticizing Robertson for failing to delay Gregg's advance. Major Henry McClellan received particular praise: if not for his quick thinking on Fleetwood Hill, Gregg's division may have seized and held the hill, thereby altering the outcome of the battle.

Robert E. Lee also praised Stuart, declaring, "the dispositions made by you to meet the strong attack of the enemy appear to have been judicious . . . the troops were well and skillfully managed, and . . . conducted themselves with marked gallantry. The result of the action calls for our grateful thanks to Almighty God, and is honorable alike to the officers and men engaged."

If Lee realized how close his cavalry division came to defeat that day, he certainly did not let on.

"This Battle Made the Federal Cavalry"

CHAPTER TWELVE

After a long day of desperate fighting, Jeb Stuart could count Brandy Station as a victory. He successfully, although narrowly, repulsed Pleasonton's expedition, keeping his force intact in the process. While the victory was not complete, Stuart could claim it by virtue of holding the field when the battle concluded and because he prevented Pleasonton from accomplishing his goal of destroying or dispersing the large concentration of Confederate cavalry that had gathered in Culpeper County.

One fact, however, could not be ignored in the midst of Stuart's victory. For nearly 14 bitter hours, the Federal troopers fought the Confederates to a standstill. Pleasonton's horsemen performed admirably that day, going toe to toe with the very best that the Confederate cavalry had to offer, and they more than held their own. Victory was within their grasp.

Pleasonton's aggressiveness waned once Buford's assault lost its momentum after Grimes Davis was killed. Additional losses in line officers in Davis' regiments following Davis' death further hindered the attack. This, along with the quick and effective reaction of the Confederates, stifled any further offensive plans that Pleasonton may have entertained. He was perfectly content to let Gregg fight it out on Fleetwood Hill alone. With Stuart's line stretched thin, Buford's wing very well could have broken through, but Pleasonton lacked the moral courage to turn Buford loose.

Alfred Duffie's failure to break through Butler's position in the valley of Mountain Run ultimately led to his transfer from the cavalry. (dd)

A view of the location of the Confederate Horse Artillery from the Beverly Ford Road. (dd)

Moreover, Pleasonton's plan was not only based on faulty intelligence, he also did not consider the possibility of finding the Confederates where he expected them to be. Also, he divided his force, preventing the knockout blow. Poor intelligence and poor planning doomed the expedition to failure. As such, Pleasonton failed in his stated mission of destroying or dispersing Stuart's force. Most importantly, Pleasonton failed to delay Lee's march north; the Army of Northern Virginia's advance toward its date with destiny in Pennsylvania began the next day instead of when it was supposed to on June 9.

Undoubtedly, the greatest impact of the battle was its effect on the morale of the Federal cavalry. Major Henry McClellan remembered that Brandy Station "made the Federal Cavalry. The fact is that up to June 9, 1863, the Confederate cavalry did have its own way . . . and the record of their success becomes almost monotonous. . . . But after that time we held our ground only by hard fighting." In fact, as Luther Hopkins of the 6th Virginia Cavalry remembered it, "Our enemies could have driven us back farther if they had tried to, but they seemed to be afraid of getting into trouble."

Federals noted the shift in power, too. "From that day forth the prestige of the Confederate cavalry was broken," claimed Capt. Wesley Merritt, who was promoted to brigadier general 19 days later, "and its pre-eminence was gone forever."

One Union officer summed it up best: "The Confederate cavalry, caught napping, endeavored to repair its fault with promptness and gallantry; it had, however, been checked upon the threshold of an aggressive movement, and its leader was taught a lesson, which sooner or later is learned by the general who undervalues his enemy."

*   *   *

During the battle, Pleasanton lost two brigade commanders, Cols. Grimes Davis and Percy Wyndham, while Col. Alfred Duffié demonstrated that he lacked the competence to command a division. Two days afterward, with lessons learned, Pleasonton reorganized his corps.

Buford remained in command of the First Division. Colonel William Gamble of the 8th Illinois Cavalry, who had been recovering from a wound received on the Peninsula in August 1862, took over for the deceased Grimes Davis. Devin continued to lead his brigade, while the Reserve Brigade, which had always served with the First Division, formally joined it. The U.S. Regulars also received a new commander in the form of Maj. Samuel H. Starr of the 6th U.S. Cavalry.

Pleasonton completely reconstituted his Second and Third Divisions. He merged them into a single command under the leadership of David Gregg.

The question of what to do with Alfred Duffié was much more complicated. He remained a senior colonel who could claim command of a brigade. To deal with the Duffié problem, Pleasonton recommended Judson Kilpatrick for a promotion to the rank of brigadier general. When the promotion came through, Kilpatrick took command of Duffié's brigade, meaning that the Frenchman reverted to command of his regiment, the 1st Rhode Island Cavalry. Probably unbeknownst to Pleasonton, Hooker had endorsed Duffié's promotion to brigadier general for his service at the battle of Kelly's Ford in March. When the commission was received, the newly promoted Duffié was transferred out of the Cavalry Corps.

At the end of the Gettysburg campaign, Pleasonton falsely claimed that he had discovered Lee's invasion plans, a claim that had little foundation in fact. His subsequent actions and communications do not

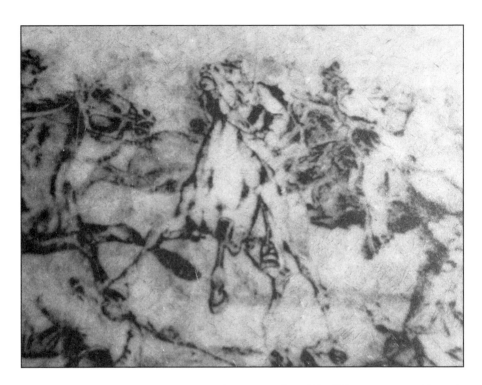

The battle of Brandy Station established the Union cavalry as an effective combat force. (cm)

support the contention. He did not capture Stuart's field desk as he claimed, and he also did not capture the Confederate commander's headquarters tent or its contents. Pleasonton simply did not do what he claimed, but lying and greatly exaggerating his own role was nothing new for him.

*   *   *

Much of the credit for the victory at Brandy Station must go to Maj. Robert F. Beckham and his resilient horse artillerists. "At every important point of the field, we have found Beckham's guns playing a leading role," the historian of the Army of Northern Virginia's artillery wrote. Their performance at St. James Church halted the initial Federal attack. The effective fire at Fleetwood Hill bought valuable time for Stuart to shift his forces to meet threats. Beckham's gunners expended hundreds of rounds during the battle. One of Chew's horse artillerists, Sgt. George Neese, remembered that his piece alone fired 160 rounds that day, burning out its breach and rendering it useless.

The Confederates also had the advantage of position. They utilized the ridges at St. James

Church, Fleetwood Hill, and Yew Ridge effectively in defending against the determined Union assaults. The Confederate cavalry held the high ground at all times during the battle, never losing control of any of it. The topography played a major role in Stuart's victory at Brandy Station.

Another key to the Confederate victory was Stuart's skillful handling of his troopers. Although he was clearly surprised that morning, Stuart responded immediately to the initial threat and directed the defenses of St. James Church and Fleetwood Hill. Seemingly everywhere at once, Stuart even pitched into the fighting himself. One of his aides, a Prussian, Maj. Heros von Borcke, remembered that upon "learning that he had been flanked and strong units were occupying his previous headquarters blocking his retreat, Stuart's strength and military genius rose to their highest." A man in the ranks recalled, "Genl Stuart always fought the hardest when things looked the worst." Stuart managed his forces well and was served extremely well by Rooney Lee, Hampton, Jones, Butler, and especially Beckham.

At the same time, however, Stuart's handling of the battle had its critics. "The cavalry fight at Brandy Station can hardly be called a victory," complained Capt. Charles Minor Blackford, serving on James Longstreet's staff. "Stuart was certainly surprised and but for the supreme gallantry of his subordinate officers and the men in his command, it would have been a day of disaster."

Another Rebel soldier wrote, "Genl Stuart was beautifully surprised and whipped the other day. . . . It is amusing to hear the cavalry fellows trying to bluff out of it." John B. Jones, a clerk in the Confederate War Department, noted in his diary, "The surprise of Stuart on the Rappahannock has chilled every heart. . . . The question is on every tongue—have the generals relaxed in vigilance? If so, sad is the prospect!"

Even the Southern press railed about Stuart's performance. The editor of the *Richmond Sentinel* proclaimed, "The fight, on the whole, may be said to have begun in a surprise and ended in a victory. The latter is what we are accustomed to hear of Confederate soldiers; the former we trust never to hear again."

The Richmond Examiner called Stuart's command "this much puffed cavalry of the Army of Northern Virginia" and pointed out that it was not the first time Stuart had been surprised in 1863: Federal cavalry caught him by surprise at Kelly's Ford on March 17.

> *If the war was a tournament, invented and supported for the pleasure and profit of a few vain and weak-headed officers, these disasters might be dismissed with compassion. But the country pays dearly for the blunders which encourage the enemy to overrun the land with a cavalry which is daily learning to despise the mounted troops of the Confederacy. It is high time that this branch of the service should be reformed.*

Implying that Lee's cavalry desperately needed a new commander, the editorial declared, "The enemy is evidently determined to employ his cavalry extensively, and has spared no pains or cost to perfect that arm. The only effective means of preventing the mischief . . . is to reorganize our own forces, enforce a stricter discipline among the men, and insist on more earnestness among the officers in the discharge of their very important duty."

This criticism infuriated Stuart, who wrote to his wife Flora, "God has spared me through another bloody battle, and blessed with victory our arms . . . the papers are in great error . . . it was no surprise, the enemys (sic) movement was known, and he was defeated. I lost no paper—no nothing—except the casualties of battle."

In spite of everything, Stuart's troopers slept in their own camps on the night of June 9, 1863. They held the battlefield after parrying Pleasonton's attempt to "destroy or disperse" his command. Even if he was surprised at the beginning of the day, Stuart won the battle while his men lived up to their vaunted reputation.

Grumble Jones and Wade Hampton had been exceptional, leading Jones to declare, "my brigade bore the brunt of action both in the morning and evening, and lost severely in killed and wounded, but had the satisfaction of seeing the enemy worsted in every particular more than ourselves." Hampton led his troopers into a breach twice that day, at St. James

Church and again on Fleetwood Hill. In particular, the Cobb Legion Cavalry distinguished itself. "We were fortunate in retaking Gen. Stuart's Hdqtrs. . . . when all eyes were turned upon us & our men behaved with gallantry and spirit," remembered its Lt. Col. Will Delony. "I would not be surprised if our charge made Young a Brigadier . . . we succeeded as I have always told you we would succeed–with such a set of men to follow. I never have seen, nor do I ever again expect to see a field swept in such splendid style, as was that battle field by Hampton's Brigade."

The same praise, however, cannot be given to either Col. Thomas Munford or Brig. Beverly Robertson. Munford delayed his movement from the Hazel River and did not arrive until the fighting was nearly over. Once he deployed his men, however, they did a fine job of driving Buford's tired troopers from the northern crest of Fleetwood Hill. Robertson's men nearly took themselves out of the fight of their own volition, firing a single volley and then clearing the way to the Confederate rear at Fleetwood Hill.

Almost immediately Robert E. Lee recognized the long-term importance of the battle and the obstacles he and Stuart now faced. On June 10, he wrote to President Jefferson Davis, noting that the Federal cavalry clearly claimed superior "numbers, resources, and all the numbers, resources, and means and appliances for carrying on the war." The Confederacy could not hope to avoid "the military consequences of a vigorous use" of those means. "We should not, therefore, conceal from ourselves that our resources in men are constantly diminishing," he observed, "and that the disproportion in this respect between us and our enemies is steadily augmenting."

In the grand scheme of things, Brandy Station may have had a great impact on the outcome of the Gettysburg campaign. Instead of most of Lee's infantry moving on June 9, the gray-clad infantry marched on June 10, meaning that the beginning of Lee's second great invasion of the North was delayed by only a single day. That single day's delay may very well have made the difference in allowing John Buford's dauntless troopers to reach and hold Gettysburg on June 30, 1863, setting the stage for one of the greatest battles on the North American continent.

"STUART WAS CERTAINLY SURPRISED AND BUT FOR THE SUPREME GALLANTRY OF HIS SUBORDINATE OFFICERS AND THE MEN IN HIS COMMAND, IT WOULD HAVE BEEN A DAY OF DISASTER."

— *Charles Minor Blackford*

The Road to Gettysburg

POSTSCRIPT

BY DANIEL T. DAVIS

The performance of the Federal cavalry at Brandy Station buoyed the spirits of Alfred Pleasonton. His dispatches following the battle effused pride in his troopers and himself. His offensive across the Rapphannock, he believed, had been enough to "prevent Stuart from making his raid . . .[in]to Maryland."

Pleasonton, however, was sorely mistaken.

Undeterred by the Union attack, Robert E. Lee was determined to adhere to his plan of steadily moving his infantry away from Fredericksburg, through Culpeper, and on to the Shenandoah Valley. Although Stuart's cavalry was roughly handled by Pleasonton's, Stuart's role in Lee's overall plan remained unchanged: His primary responsibility was to screen the infantry movement west.

Surprisingly, despite the battle on June 9 and his close proximity to the enemy, Pleasonton soon lost contact with the Confederates. While he continued to send back unsubstantiated reports to Maj. Gen. Joseph Hooker, he did not possess clear insight into Lee's movements or intentions. By the middle of June, Hooker was convinced *something* was afoot, but he didn't know what. Enemy infantry had gradually left his front at Fredericksburg. On the fourteenth, he abandoned his own lines and began to move north to keep pace with the enemy and to shield Washington. Hooker's infantry followed the Orange and Alexandria Railroad toward Catlett's Station and Centreville.

Munford's troopers defended this position along the Snickersville Turnpike against repeated Union charges. Col. Calvin Douty, commander of the 1st Maine Cavalry, is thought to have fallen in the area near the tree on the right.
(dd)

Stuart established his headquarters at the Rod Fox Inn in Middleburg on June 17 before he was driven out by the appearance of the 1st Rhode Island Cavalry. Today, the building serves as a restaurant and bed and breakfast. (dd)

In conjunction with the infantry, Pleasonton pulled his troopers away from the Rappahannock and concentrated around Manassas.

Two days after Hooker began his march, Stuart left Culpeper. His main objective was to shield Lt. Gen. James Longstreet's corps as it moved northwest toward the town of Winchester. A crucial part of Stuart's mission was to guard the gaps in the Blue Ridge Mountains. Of particular importance were the Little River and Snickersville Turnpikes. The two thoroughfares ran from the Blue Ridge in the west toward the Bull Run Mountains in the east and directly toward the Union concentration.

It was imperative that Stuart retain control over these roads lest the prying Federal cavalry reach the mountain passes and discover Lee's army. This gave significant importance to the country between the two ranges. Known as the Loudoun Valley, the area consisted of a series of rolling hills that made the terrain perfect for defensive tactics. Within the valley and along the Little River Turnpike were three small villages. The easternmost village was situated on the Little River and was known as Aldie. Just several miles to the west was Middleburg. Beyond that and at the base of the Blue Ridge was Upperville. These villages would lend their names to the battles to come.

By the night of June 16, Hooker was fed up by the lack of verifiable intelligence from his cavalry chief. Orders were promptly issued to Pleasonton. "The Commanding General relies upon you with your cavalry force to give him information of where the enemy is, his force, and his movements," it read. "You have a sufficient cavalry force to do this. Drive in pickets, if necessary and get us information. It is better that we should lose men than to be without knowledge of the enemy." The next morning, Pleasonton dispatched Brig. Gen. David Gregg's division west along the Little River Turnpike in an effort to locate the Confederates.

As Gregg's troopers moved out, Stuart rode into the village of Middleburg. He had brought with him the brigades of Cols. Thomas Munford and John Chambliss and Brig. Gen. Beverly Robertson. Chambliss had taken over Rooney Lee's command after Lee was wounded at Brandy Station atop Yew Ridge. Keeping Robertson's brigade with him, Stuart sent Munford and Chambliss east along the Little River Turnpike.

The opposing sides collided at Aldie. Leading Gregg's advance was Brig. Gen. Judson Kilpatrick. Fresh from his recent fight atop Fleetwood Hill, Kilpatrick engaged elements from Munford's brigade and quickly pushed them back through the town. Munford withdrew and split his brigade to cover both the Little River and Snickersville Turnpikes. To counter the Confederates, Kilpatrick brought up and deployed Lt. Alanson Randol's Battery E/G of the 1st U.S. Artillery on a knoll near the intersection of the two roads. Randol's immediate threat came from the 5th Virginia. After an initial attack by the 2nd New York was repulsed, a squadron from the 6th Ohio arrived and, together with the Empire Staters, pushed back the Virginians.

With the retreat of the Virginians, the fighting shifted to the north along the Snickersville Turnpike. There, Munford had deployed on high ground behind a stone wall. His position was hidden by a sharp bend in the pike. Repeated attacks by squadrons from the 4th New York and 1st Massachusetts failed to dislodge

Union and Confederate troopers clashed at Aldie during the turbulent cavalry actions on the road to Gettysburg. (loc)

the Confederates. The 1st Massachusetts suffered severely. "I do not hesitate to say that I have never seen as many Yankees killed in the same space of ground in any fight I have ever seen," Munford wrote after the battle. The failed assaults left Randol's battery vulnerable, and Munford ordered a counterattack. As the charging Confederates approached, Kilpatrick committed his last regiment, the 1st Maine, to the fight. Led by Col. Calvin Douty, the regiment charged and pushed Munford back to the stone wall. Douty fell dead in the charge but his men managed to secure the artillery. As night fell over the field, Munford quietly pulled back to the west.

Stuart, meanwhile, had been forced out of Middleburg. While the battle had raged at Aldie, Gregg sent Col. Alfred Duffié and the 1st Rhode Island on a flanking mission to the south. The Rhode Islanders surprised Stuart and his staff, who beat a hasty retreat to Rector's Crossroads. Perhaps in an effort to redeem himself for his poor performance at Brandy Station, Duffié, unsupported and isolated, decided to remain near Middleburg. It was a poor decision. Ruffled by his sudden flight, Stuart sent Robertson's North Carolinians in search of the Rhode Islanders. Robertson easily pushed the Federals out of Middleburg.

The 1st Massachusetts Cavalry lost 198 of the 294 troopers engaged at the battle of Aldie. In 1881, veterans of the regiment returned to the battlefield to dedicate this monument, which stands near the Confederate position they so desperately tried to capture. (dd)

Unfortunately, as Duffié attempted to make his

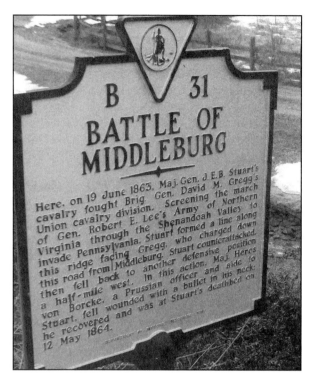

Located just beyond the hilltop's crest, a historical marker for the battle of Middleburg stands atop Mount Defiance. (dd)

way back to Union lines, he ran into the 9th Virginia Cavalry. This second fight escalated into a rout, and the entire regiment was nearly lost. Demoralized, Duffié limped into Centreville on the afternoon of June 18.

Stuart, however, still had reason to be optimistic. Reinforcements were expected shortly from the brigades of Brig. Gens. Wade Hampton and William "Grumble" Jones. Moreover, he held a new position west of Middleburg along high ground known as Mount Defiance. The name was appropriate, for on the morning of June 19, Pleasonton resumed his advance. Gregg's division once again led the way along the Little River Turnpike. Similar to Duffié's earlier effort to turn the Confederate line, Brig. Gen. John Buford's division advanced to the north in the hopes of flanking Stuart's position.

Gregg immediately encountered stiff resistance from Chambliss and Robertson. Supported by the batteries of Capts. Marcellus Moorman and William McGregor, the Confederate artillery poured down a heavy fire from Mount Defiance. Although Gregg's men made some headway against Robertson's regiments on the right, the Confederates did not budge. To the north, Buford encountered elements from Munford's brigade. The old dragoon also ran into stiff resistance and was unable to flank the Rebel position. Stuart had skillfully handled his troopers at Middleburg even though he was outnumbered. Hard pressed, he abandoned Mount Defiance.

June 20 greeted the hard-fighting troopers with a thunderstorm. More importantly, Hampton and Jones arrived to bolster the Confederates. Stuart decided to place Hampton in support of Robertson along the Little River—or Ashby's Gap Turnpike, as it was called—to the west of Middleburg, while Jones reinforced Chambliss and Munford. The addition of these brigades was beneficial against the relentless Federals. While Stuart's men had been pressed out of Aldie and Middleburg, they had delayed the Union cavalry and successfully shielded them from the Blue Ridge. Now, Stuart assumed a new position on the eastern outskirts of Upperville.

Inspired by the events of the last four days, Pleasonton planned on one more push for the morning of June 21. His plan remained unchanged. Buford was to hammer away at the Confederate's northern flank while Gregg continued his advance on Stuart's center.

Again, Kilpatrick led Gregg's advance. This time, the Union troopers encountered elements from Robertson's and Hampton's brigades. When Robertson was pushed back, Hampton moved to confront Kilpatrick, and a seesaw fight erupted between the Jeff Davis Legion and the 4th New York. Both sides pumped more regiments into the fray as Kilpatrick gained the upper hand. "Little Kil" sent the 6th Ohio in a charge down through the village. They were met by Robertson's reformed troopers, who sent them reeling back to the rear.

While Gregg and Hampton jabbed and parried, Buford himself encountered a stubborn defense. Fresh off his duel with Rooney Lee, Capt. Wesley Merritt's men "attacked the enemy vigorously, driving him successfully from many strong positions. The work was difficult, and cost much severe fighting, the country being well adapted to defense, because of its hilly character and the long lines of substantial stone walls and heavy woods which covered it."

The only infantry fighting in the Loudoun Valley took place here at Goose Creek Bridge. Frustrated by Stuart's stubborn defense, Pleasonton called upon Col. Strong Vincent's brigade to seize the crossing. Elements from the 16th Michigan Infantry advanced from the high ground opposite the bridge, crossed Goose Creek, and successfully drove off the Confederate cavalry. Vincent and his men would achieve everlasting fame less than a month later when they participated in the defense of Little Round Top at Gettysburg. (dd)

Gradually, Buford was able to push back the Confederates. He moved Col. William Gamble's brigade cross-country through a sunken road to a position near the Trappe Road. A north-south thoroughfare, the Trappe Road branched off the Ashby's Gap Turnpike behind Hampton's position. If

The Blue Ridge Mountains look down on part of the Upperville battlefield, where John Buford's division traded blows with regiments from Grumble Jones's brigade. (dd)

Buford captured the intersection, both Hampton and Robertson would be cut off and surrounded.

Buford immediately sent Gamble's brigade forward. Gamble's troopers ran into the 2nd North Carolina and Cap. Roger Chew's battery. Engaged by the 3rd Indiana along with the 8th and 12th Illinois, Chew retreated to a new position as the 12th Virginia Infantry, from Grumble Jones' brigade, arrived and pushed Gamble back. Undeterred, Gamble counterattacked, with some of his men fighting dismounted. Jones committed more regiments to the fight and once again repulsed the Federals. Running out of steam, Gamble decided not to press the attack. Below them, despite heavy hand-to-hand fighting, Hampton's and Robertson's troopers managed to hold the crucial road junction. As darkness descended across the Blue Ridge, Gregg and Buford broke off the fight.

Ironically, the battle had the same impact on Pleasonton as an episode at Brandy Station did less than two weeks earlier. After the initial Union success of crossing Beverly Ford, Pleasonton balked in front of Stuart's line at St. James Church. While he had managed to press the Confederates out of Aldie and Middleburg, Pleasonton once again showed his skittishness after their determined stand at Upperville. On June 22, he ordered his divisions back to the east and effectively ended the fighting for the Loudoun Valley. Pleasonton could claim a tactical victory, but he had failed to locate Lee's infantry, let alone delay its progress. By the time the action in the Loudon Valley wrapped up, Lee's Second Corps was spread out through Maryland in anticipation of moving into Pennsylvania, while his Third Corps was marching into the northern end of the Shenandoah Valley, followed by his First Corps.

In reaction, Hooker also continued his march north, though he remained largely blind. On June 25, he set his army in motion across the Potomac at Edward's Ferry and into Maryland, unsure of what awaited him there.

As well as Stuart had performed during the Loudon Valley cavalry clashes, his achievement mattered very little on a personal level. The sting of criticism from Brandy Station still lingered. Within days after Upperville, Stuart would leave the valley on another expedition that carried him and the two armies toward a volatile confrontation in Pennsylvania.

The Four Battles of Brandy Station

APPENDIX A
BY ERIC J. WITTENBERG

Although the great struggle on June 9, 1863, is the best-remembered cavalry battle that took place in and around Culpeper, Virginia, during the Civil War, it was not the only major cavalry battle fought on the slopes of Fleetwood Hill. In fact, the June 9, 1863, fight was actually the second battle of Brandy Station. And there were two more that came after it.

The first battle of Brandy Station occurred on August 20, 1862. That day, Jeb Stuart's cavalry led the way for the Army of Northern Virginia, which was headed for the Rappahannock River crossings north of the town of Culpeper. Fitzhugh Lee's brigade led James Longstreet's infantry through Stevensburg toward Kelly's Ford. Beverly Robertson, then commanding the brigade that Grumble Jones commanded in June 1863, led Jackson's infantry north toward Rappahannock Station. A brigade of federal cavalry commanded by Brig. Gen. George D. Bayard awaited the Confederate horsemen at Fleetwood Hill.

The center of Bayard's line of battle rested on Fleetwood Hill near the Miller house. Two of his regiments—the 1st New Jersey Cavalry, commanded by Polish immigrant Col. Joseph Karge, and the 2nd New York Cavalry, commanded by Judson Kilpatrick—sat astride the southern crest of Fleetwood Hill, holding precisely the same ground where they fought the following June. Bayard's brigade also included the 1st Pennsylvania Cavalry, which also fought on Fleetwood Hill the next June.

Robertson spotted the Union horsemen waiting for him. "As soon as practicable I ordered a charge, and led the Twelfth Virginia Regiment directly against the center of their line, while the Sixth and Seventh were directed against their flank," he reported. "The men charged gallantly, and after a brief hand-to-hand contest the enemy was routed with the loss of several killed and a

OPPOSITE: The Orange and Alexandria Railroad facilitated movement for both armies when they operated east of the Blue Ridge, eyeing the westernmost fords across the Rapidan and Rappahannock Rivers. That made places along the rail line—like Brandy Station—hotspots for fighting as the armies used it as an avenue for advance and retreat. (dd)

number wounded, capturing 64 prisoners, including several commissioned officers. Our loss was 3 killed and 13 wounded."

The two regiments that Robertson used to turn Bayard's flanks—the 6th and 7th Virginia Cavalry— of course played a major role on June 9. On August 20, 1862, Maj. Cabel Fluornoy commanded the 6th Virginia, just as he did on June 9, while Grumble Jones, still a colonel at the time, commanded the 7th Virginia Cavalry that day. Colonel Asher W. Harman commanded the 12th Virginia Cavalry at both battles.

Unlike his performance on June 9, Robertson handled his troopers in praiseworthy fashion that day. "General Robertson had cause to be proud of the command which his superior discipline, organization, and drill had brought to the stability of veterans," wrote Stuart of Robertson's performance.

Although none of the Union units engaged left reports of the August 20 fight, it nevertheless was significant because it marked the first brigade vs. brigade combat between Union and Confederate cavalry in the Eastern Theater of the Civil War. These units came to know each other very well, and they clashed on the same ground nine months later.

The June 9 fight was the opening engagement of the Gettysburg campaign, which was bracketed by fierce cavalry fights for possession of Fleetwood Hill. On August 1, 1863, after the armies had returned to the banks of the Rappahannock River from whence they began the Gettysburg Campaign. Early on the morning of August 1, John Buford's First Cavalry Division splashed across the Rappahannock and made a beeline for Brandy Station. Wade Hampton's brigade—then commanded by Col. Laurence S. Baker of the 2nd North Carolina Cavalry while Hampton recuperated from the serious combat wound he sustained at Gettysburg on July 3—responded to the threat. Accompanied by at least a battery and an additional section of Confederate horse artillery, Baker headed northeast along the railroad track and drew his brigade up in line of battle perpendicular to the track of the Orange & Alexandria. He placed his artillery on the left of the line, just north of the railroad tracks. The gunners then opened the battle, drawing steady and accurate return fire from the Union horse artillerists.

The battle on Fleetwood Hill, August 1862. (loc)

Buford then attacked, driving Young's men almost all the way back to Culpeper. The retreat became a series of stands and withdrawals: Baker's men would make a stand, and then be driven back. At one point, Buford's troopers nearly encircled the gray-clad horsemen, and only deadly work with canister at a range of 50 yards by Capt. James Hart's battery halted the blue-clad cavalry and gave Baker's troopers the chance to escape.

"[A] large body of federal Cavalry crossed the Rappahannock and attacked us," a Confederate gunner recalled, "and pressed us back slowly towards Culpeper court house. The day was very hot. At a point about a mile south of Brandy station, being pressed very closely, and in danger of being overwhelmed by numbers, both in front and on the left flank, we gave them canister and very short range. The order was given, 'a double charge,' and for the first time (according to my memory) we loaded a double charge, and let them have it. This repulsed them and give us time to 'limber to the rear.'"

As Baker's hard-pressed troopers neared Culpeper, infantry from Maj. Gen. Richard H. Anderson's division of Longstreet's Corps "came to our help, and the tide of battle was reversed and the enemy driven across the river."

Baker was badly wounded in the arm and had to turn over command to Col. Pierce M. B. Young of the Cobb Legion Cavalry—until Young was also wounded. Command then devolved upon Col. John L. Black of the 1st North Carolina Cavalry.

Only the timely arrival of Grumble Jones and his brigade, bearing down on the Federal flank, and the addition of another battery of Confederate horse artillery caused Buford to break off and withdraw. The tables were turned—Buford had to conduct a fighting withdrawal himself—until darkness finally ended the Confederate pursuit. Buford suffered 22 killed, 95 wounded, and 157 missing in the day's hard fighting. Stuart lost 75-100 killed and wounded and another 50 missing that day, including every colonel in Baker's brigade.

Buford got the best of the day's combat, establishing a solid bridgehead on the south bank of the Rappahannock River while also confirming the presence of the Army of Northern Virginia's infantry in the area. His success permitted the Army of the Potomac to cross the Rappahannock and secure the area. Buford's success in the third battle of Brandy Station had significant consequences.

The fourth battle of Brandy Station occurred on October 11, 1863. The Army of the Potomac had been operating south of Culpeper since September, but an offensive by the Army of Northern Virginia was slowly shoving it back. That morning, John Buford and his First Cavalry Division were to cross the Rapidan River and then pull back north of the Rappahannock. In a running fight that began at Raccoon Ford on the Rapidan, Buford pulled back to the vicinity of Brandy Station, where he intended to link up with Judson Kilpatrick's Third Cavalry Division.

When Kilpatrick's division arrived and formed up, the two divisions of Union cavalry occupied Fleetwood Hill, their line of battle extending across it. Before long, four batteries of Union horse artillery bristled on the hill, which offered an intimidating front to Jeb Stuart's cavalry, which was forming for an attack upon near Brandy Station. Stuart attempted to flank the blue-clad horsemen from their strong position on Fleetwood Hill by moving off to the northwest in the direction of St. James Church, but by then, darkness was falling. With the Union wagons safely across the Rappahannock, Buford and Kilpatrick began to withdraw from the field with Stuart pressing his left flank. The cover of darkness allowed the federal cavalry to escape after a long and very difficult day of fighting. The last major engagement fought on Fleetwood Hill ended.

In addition to the four major battles, guerrillas of Maj. John Singleton Mosby's 43rd Battalion of Virginia Cavalry pounced on Union rearguard troops near the base of Fleetwood Hill on November 26, 1863, during the Mine Run Campaign. Leaving 40 Union wagons burning, Mosby's men escaped with 23 prisoners, 112 mules, and 7 horses at the cost of one man wounded, and Mosby's horse wounded also. "Mosby's Culpeper Raid" was a success.

Thus, four major cavalry battles occurred on the lovely, verdant slopes of Fleetwood Hill. Another eight distinct engagements occurred on Fleetwood Hill between the first one on August 20, 1862 and November 8, 1863, at the beginning of the Mine Run Campaign. With twelve separate engagements having been fought on Fleetwood Hill, it earned the title of the most fought-over piece of ground in North America.

The Winter Encampment

APPENDIX B
BY MIKE BLOCK

By December 4, 1863, the Army of the Potomac returned to Culpeper County following the Mine Run Campaign. Army Commander Maj. Gen. George Gordon Meade established his headquarters on the eastern slope of Fleetwood Hill, the center of his army. He had further increased the confidence of his men by not needlessly sending them against the formidable Confederate earthworks along the Mine Run.

He arranged his five corps to protect the army and its single supply line, the Orange and Alexandria (O&A) Railroad. Major General John Newton's I Corps centered in the town of Culpeper and stretched southward to Cedar Mountain. Major General Gouvernour K. Warren, leading the II Corps, camped between the villages of Stevensburg and Brandy Station, with brigades forward near Morton's and Germanna Fords. The III Corps, led by Maj. Gen. William French, camped around Brandy Station. Major General John Sedgewick's VI Corps was located along the Hazel River at Welford Ford. Major General George Sykes V Corps drew the unenviable task of guarding the O&A from the likes of John Mosby and other guerrillas. His divisions stretched from Rappahannock Station to Manassas Junction.

Meade's three cavalry divisions were similarly scattered, defending and picketing the forward edges of the army. Two divisions were located in Culpeper, and the third wintered in Fauquier County.

Nearly 100,000 soldiers spent between December 1863 and May 1864 in Culpeper, Fauquier, and Prince William counties. The soldiers built cabins, typically housing four men each; NCOs and officers less. Hospitals were established for

The Graffiti House, one of the best-known landmarks of the Brandy Station battlefield, was built circa 1858 near the railroad tracks, which made it a prominent structure during the winter of 1863-64. The second-floor walls are covered in scribbles left by soldiers—such as the sketch of a girl (opposite)—hence the house name. According to the Brandy Station Foundation, which now owns the house and uses it as a musuem, "The graffiti could have been made by soldiers recuperating in the hospital, by other soldiers posted at Brandy Station, or by soldiers passing through the town." (cm)

each divisional. Chapels and entertainment halls were constructed. A city of sutlers, photographers, eating establishments and other providers of wears popped up around the camps, but especially around the growing supply depot at Brandy Station. There were nearly 50,000 cabins, stables, and other structures built during this period.

Joseph Martin, a artillerist in the 6th New York Independent Battery, described the Brandy Station landscape in February 1864: "The immense plain of Brandy Station is completely beset with log cabins . . . Already extensive forests . . . have begun to melt before the legion axes in the hands of sturdy soldiery. . . . Regiments and brigades, which in the first days of December encamped in the midst of thick woods, stand far out upon that plain surrounded by stumps."

The army consumed any resource it could, including timber, fences, livestock, and crops. Culpeper citizens watched as "neighborhood churches, fences, outbuildings, slave quarters and the unoccupied houses of absent neighbors [were] torn down for their lumber." Cabins and tents were also adorned with doors, repurposed for the Army of the Potomac.

Top: **Wellford Ford, with a Federal camp in the distance.**

Bottom: **The ford today.** (loc)(mb)

Once the camps were established, routine became the order of the day. Soldiers not required for picket stood in morning formations and participated in camp details that maintained discipline and order. There was little drilling among the veterans until late in the spring. The conscripts drilled and drilled, though. A Vermont private wrote, "There is quite a lot of new recruits in the Regt now, 5 from [Preston] are here. Cummings Hale's boy, Mr. Nutting is pretty sick, where did they find that specimen of Raw Material for a soldier. Some of the new recruits have got the measles they drill now twice a day. [W]e ain't drill in about 7 weeks, except the drill down across the Rapidan and back"

Sickness in camp was common. For most of the soldiers who had already spent a winter in the field, camp disease was not an issue, although accidents were. For the recruits, measles, pneumonia and various camp fevers took their toll. More than 1100 soldiers died, mostly from disease, during the encampment.

Some casualties were due to combat. On February 6, 1864, elements of the II Corps crossed the Rapidan in a wasted feint against the rebels so Maj. Gen. Benjamin Butler could raid Richmond. Butler never started, but the II Corps soldiers suffered 255 killed and wounded. In late February, Maj. Gen. Judson Kilpatrick attempted to raid Richmond; again, the only result for the Federals was loss of life.

Seven of the deaths were the result of execution. Six of the unfortunate privates were executed by firing squad for desertion: Winslow Allen, 76th New York Infantry, George Blowers, 2nd Vermont Infantry, William Devoe, 57th New York Infantry, Cyrus Hunter, 3rd Maine Infantry, John McMann, 11th U.S. Infantry, and John Teague, 5th Vermont. The sixth soldier, Thomas Dawson of the 20th Massachusetts, was hung. His crime was drunkenness and an assault on an old woman. Father William Corby, of Gettysburg and Notre Dame fame, was the attending priest. Corby wrote, "the provost marshal misjudged the length of the rope being used. When the trapdoor sprung [Dawson] fell to a standing position on the ground. A frantic executioner seized the end of the rope and jerked the prisoner upward until death slowly came."

Organized activities were begun. Chapels were built, with canvas roofs supplied by the Christian Commission.

TOP: Rows of tents lined up in a Federal camp near Brandy Station. (loc)

BOTTOM: One of many Federal hospitals constructed during the encampment. (loc)

"Tonight we dedicated our new chapel and . . . have named it 'Hope' Chapel," one soldier wrote. "The building is made of logs hewn smooth on one side and built up cob fashion. The roof is covered by a large canvas, presented by the Christian Commission." When not a chapel, the building held a variety of activities including Temperance meetings, debates, spelling schools, free mason meetings and lectures.

Activities and entertainment were found outside the cabins, as well. Men swam in the Hazel and Rappahannock Rivers. Soldiers conducted target practice, raced horses and played baseball. They also built auditoriums that were venues for plays, concerts, lectures, and lyceums. The 4th Michigan went on a hunt: "Boys turned out for a 'Grand Hunt' on the 'Rats'

The II Corps's Washington Day ball (above) was a far cry from the winter misery they had endured during the Army of the Potomac's "Valley Forge" winter of 1862-63 in nearby Stafford County. (loc)

among the rubbish, killed about 60 rats old and young."

Visitors arrived in camp. Wives of the officers travelled to Culpeper and spent 20 days with their husbands. Most of the guests had their visits extended two or three times. In addition to riding through the camps and countryside, they visited the signal station atop Mount Pony to see the Confederate camps across the Rapidan River. Then, there were parties.

Nearly every division and many brigades held some kind of gala during the winter. Most notable was the Washington Birthday Ball hosted by the II Corps. The hall was enormous. "We planned and built a building 80X40, with two immense fireplaces on one side large enough to take in logs ten feet long . . . decorated handsomely with evergreens, flags, guidons, various kinds of small arms, drums, etc." The ball was the social event of the season. Besides the officers and their ladies, dignitaries from the north travelled to Brandy Station. Among the guests were "Vice-President (Hannibal) Hamlin, Governor and Mrs. Kate (Chase) Sprague, of Rhode Island, the wife of Governor Andrew Curtain of Pennsylvania, at least two U. S. Senators (Hale of New Hampshire and Wilkinson of Minnesota), Supreme Court Justice Samuel Miller and his wife, a large party from the British Embassy, plus hundreds of others." On the day following the ball, the II Corps and Kilpatrick's cavalry division conducted a review for the dignitaries and guests.

Parties were not on the minds of the common soldier. The soldiers who enlisted in 1861 for three years would have their terms expiring in the spring, and there was a push to re-enlist these experienced men. The incentive was big: a 30-day furlough home in exchange for three more years of the war. They would wear a stripe on their sleeve, denoting their status as part of a veteran regiment. Rumor of the furlough had circulated since late summer, and army leadership began to press the men after they returned from Mine Run.

Since joining the army, the soldiers had seen unimaginable carnage and had lived through horrible conditions. Still, many units reenlisted in near total. They understood what was before them and what must be done.

TOP: Provost Marshall Marsena Patrick and his staff in camp. (loc)

BOTTOM: The site of Patrick's camp today. (mb)

Reasons vary as to why a soldier reenlisted. Many re-upped only for the opportunity to return home for 30 days. Others, recalling the experiences of the spring and summer of 1863, knew what the upcoming campaign would entail and decided to see the task to the end. Others chose not to, and their terms were to expire in summer.

Then there was the bonus money. Members of the 20th Indiana were to receive "$802.00 bounty and a month's pay in advance." Adelbert Knight, of the 11th United States Infantry, wrote, "We are to receive the $100 bounty for ouir [sic] first enlistment, 60 days furlough and $450 bounty for 5 years. $100 down and the rest yearly." The final amount depended on what state and local municipalities could afford to add the bounty.

As the weather warmed, drilling increased and the men began participating in reviews. Brigade and division reviews became common-place, attended by corps leadership. Corps reviews took place, observed

This area around the Clover Hill Farm was used as an encampment by the Army of the Potomac's cavalry corps in the winter of 1863-1864. (dd)

by Lt. Gen. U. S. Grant, now commander of all the Federal armies. Grant chose to make his headquarters with the Army of the Potomac, although Meade would remain in command of the army.

Coinciding with Grant's arrival was a complete reorganization of the army. After the devastating losses in 1863, Meade wished to consolidate his army. The I Corps and III Corps were eliminated—though the men were allowed to retain their distinctive badges—and merged into the II and VI Corps. Newton and French were out as corps commanders. Major General Winfield Scott Hancock returned from his wound to reassume command of the II Corps. Warren replaced Sykes, who left for Kansas. Sedgwick remained in command of the VI Corps. Meade's Cavalry had a new commander, as well. Major General Alfred Pleasonton was replaced by Maj. Gen. Phil Sheridan.

By the end of April, Meade's army numbered 104,000 and was prepared for the campaign, ready to move forward with a clear understanding of what they needed to do. They would also have Maj. Gen. Ambrose Burnside's IX Corps—19,000 more rifles—joining them.

Part of IX Corps consisted of the division of Brig. Gen. Edward Ferrero—seven regiments of United States Colored Troops (USCTs). USCTs had already been present in other Federal armies, but these were the first to become attached to the Army of the

Potomac. It would be the first time Robert E. Lee's Army of Northern Virginia would face former slaves.

Travelling with Meade would be another proven leader: Grant. At the onset of what was to become the Overland Campaign, a reporter asked Grant how long it would take him to get to Richmond. Grant replied, "I will agree to be there in about four days—that is, if General Lee becomes a party to the agreement; but if he objects, the trip will undoubtedly be prolonged." How long would it take the Army of the Potomac to get to Richmond and how the relationship between him and Meade would unfold was yet to be seen.

But the army, at least, was ready to move forward—reorganized and recommitted to the task before it following their winter encampment in Culpeper County.

MICHAEL BLOCK, *a retired Air Force Intelligence Analyst, currently works for Booz Allen Hamilton. He is the vice-president of the Friends of Cedar Mountain Battlefield and is currently gathering material for a book-length study of Rappahannock Station.*

The Battle of Kelly's Ford
The First Federal Foray Across the Rappahannock

APPENDIX C
BY DANIEL T. DAVIS

The mounted blue troopers fanned out from the river. Despite the stiff enemy resistance and rapid current, Brig. Gen. William W. Averell's men had forced a crossing of the Rappahannock at Kelly's Ford. "My command was drawn up so as to meet the enemy in every direction as fast as it crossed," Averell wrote, "and pickets pushed out on the roads running from the ford."

It was St. Patrick's Day, 1863, and the Union general had his mind set on redemption.

In late February, Averell's old friend Brig. Gen. Fitzhugh Lee had attacked his pickets at Hartwood Church. Lee pushed Averell's troopers back several miles before he ran into Union infantry and called off the attack. As he withdrew, Lee left behind a surgeon to care for his wounded. The doctor also carried a note for Averell.

Dear Averell:

Please let this surgeon assist in taking care of my wounded. I ride a pretty fast horse, but I think yours can beat mine. I wish you'd quit your shooting and get out of my State and go home. If you won't go home, why don't you come pay me a visit. Send me over a bag of coffee. Good-bye, Fitz.

The taunt embarrassed Averell and infuriated his superior, Maj. Gen. Joseph Hooker. Recently appointed to command the Army of the Potomac, one of Hooker's first acts was to consolidate his mounted units into one corps under one commander. Hooker

Although there is a John Pelham monument next to the Graffiti House at Brandy Station, this monument stands in the area where Pelham actually fell on the Kelly's Ford battlefield. It is located in the Chester F. Phelps Wildlife Area. It can be accessed from the parking area on Route 674 (Kelly's Ford Road). To reach the monument, follow the trail into the woods from the parking area. When the trail forks, keep to the right and the monument will be up ahead on the left. It is roughly 300 yards from the parking lot. Due to the nature of the terrain, the monument may only be reached seasonally. Please exercise caution and be mindful of snakes, ticks, and other wildlife. (dd)

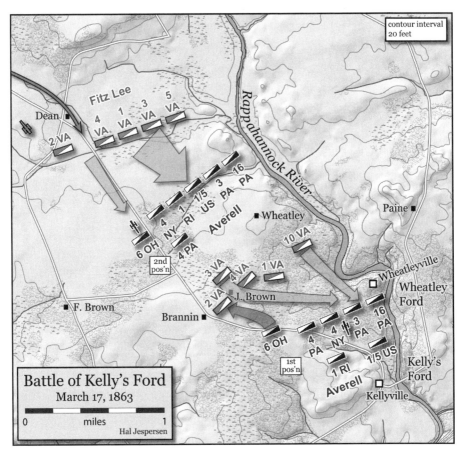

BATTLE OF KELLY'S FORD—After crossing the Rappahannock at Kelly's Ford, Averell's division advanced toward Culpeper. Met by Fitzhugh Lee's brigade, the Union troopers held their ground against the first Confederate attacks, eventually forcing Lee back to a new position. Averell resumed his advance, only to be met by Lee a second time. Once again, the blue troopers held their ground against enemy attacks. Darkness finally brought an end to the fighting.

thought this new structure, which mirrored that of the Confederates, could help improve the overall efficiency of the branch. The surprise at Hartwood Church did not bode well for arm's future operations.

Anxious for a chance to even the score with Lee, Averell requested permission from Hooker to strike back. On March 14, Hooker ordered Averell to move up the Rappahannock, cross it, and attack Lee at Culpeper Court House.

Averell's column moved out two days later. His division consisted of two brigades. The first, commanded by Col. Alfred Duffié, consisted of the 4th New York, 6th Ohio, and 1st Rhode Island. The 3rd Pennsylvania, 4th Pennsylvania, and the 16th

Pennsylvania, led by Col. John McIntosh, comprised Averell's second brigade. The division was supported by the 1st U.S. Cavalry and three squadrons from the 5th U.S. Cavalry, commanded by Captain Marcus A. Reno. The 6th New York Light Independent Battery accompanied the troopers to provide artillery support.

After a long day's march, the column bedded down in the hamlet of Morrisville while Averell's scouts continued on to Mount Holly Church. From there, they reported signs of a Confederate camp near Rappahannock Station, just east of Culpeper. Rather than marching to Rappahannock Station the next morning, Averell decided to turn directly toward the Rappahannock from his present position and cross the river at Kelly's Ford.

At 4 a.m. on the morning of March 17, the Yankees saddled up and rode toward the ford.

Elements from the 2nd and 4th Virginia Cavalry were positioned there to oppose an enemy crossing. The Virginians put up a stiff resistance until troopers from Duffié's 1st Rhode Island and 6th Ohio were finally able to force a crossing and gain possession of the south bank. The Confederates withdrew in the face of the Federal push. Around noon—and after he watered his horses—Reno began his advance toward Culpeper.

Word of the Yankees at Kelly's Ford was not long in reaching Fitzhugh Lee at Culpeper. He mounted his five Virginia cavalry regiments and rode off to meet his foe. Major General J.E.B. Stuart and Stuart's chief of artillery, Maj. John Pelham, also accompanied Lee. For the upcoming battle, Stuart decided to act as an observer and leave the tactical decisions to Lee. Arriving on the field, the gray troopers were greeted by the sight of Averell's advancing division.

Lee initiated the action and sent a dismounted squadron forward to probe the Union lines. Averell countered by sending forward the 4th New York and 4th Pennsylvania on foot along his left. John McIntosh sent the 16th Pennsylvania to extend the line to the right in an attempt to squeeze off Lee's troopers, who had taken up position behind a stone wall. The Pennsylvanian's commander, Col. J. Irvin Gregg, wrote "I dismounted the balance of my command threw my entire force some 300 yards in advance . . . and drove the enemy from the position."

To counter Averell's advance, Lee sent the 3rd Virginia and 5th Virginia forward in a mounted

Constructed in 1858, Hartwood Church was, said one Union soldier, a "lovely little backwoods chapel." The skirmish here in late February, 1863, precipitated the Union foray across the Rappahannock the following month. This house of worship remains in operation today. (dd)

charge. Major Pelham joined the Virginians in their assault. As he rode forward, a piece of shrapnel struck him, entering the back of his skull. Carried from the field, the young Alabaman passed away quietly the next morning in Culpeper.

"They cried out lustily," an officer from the 3rd Pennsylvania recalled of the Virginians, "and fired their pistols at our people." The Federals stubbornly held their position and repulsed the Confederate attack. In an effort to follow up their success, Duffié led the 1st Rhode Island and

This view looks out from the Confederate lines at Kelly's Ford. Lee's troopers struck the center and right of Averell's position, which was located in the far tree line, late in the battle. (dd)

elements of the 4th Pennsylvania and 6th Ohio into the fray. Two squadrons from Reno's 5th U.S. Cavalry joined in, and a saber-swinging melee ensued. To meet the Yankees, Lee personally led the 1st Virginia, 2nd Virginia, and 4th Virginia in a counterattack. Undeterred by Lee's charge and wishing to help their comrades, additional troopers from the 1st Rhode Island, 6th Ohio and 5th U.S. rode to Duffié's defense. This extra weight helped to blunt Lee's advance, and the Confederates were forced to fall back and regroup.

With his regiments scattered, Averell also paused to reform. After getting his men back in position, he advanced his entire division. Lee planned to meet this movement with another assault. He decided to send the 1st Virginia, 3rd Virginia, and 5th Virginia against the Union right. At the same time, the 2nd Virginia and 4th Virginia were to assail Averell's left.

Lee's front was "masked by his sharpshooters, deployed in a heavy line, and they soon commenced advancing and firing rapidly," a Pennsylvania officer recalled. "Under cover of this he was seen moving forward his main line, and preparing for a charge with a very large part of his command. . . . [A]ll felt that the great struggle of the day was about to commence."

"The enemy . . . advanced upon both flanks with great steadiness," Averell remembered. "They were at once repulsed on the right. The squadrons to form the left were shifted from the right of road under a terrific fire of shot, shell and small arms . . . bore down on my left flank." Here, the New York artillerists lent their firepower to the action "with damaging effect." To help support the guns, the 1st Rhode Island, 6th Ohio, and elements of the Regulars charged. The two lines collided, the Federals eventually gained the upper hand, and Virginians were forced to retreat.

By now, daylight had started to fade, and Averell weighed his options. He had received a report of Confederate infantry lurking nearby late in the fight. While the information proved to be false, he also considered the state of his horses, which were "very much exhausted." Rather than continue the fight, Averell "deemed it proper to withdraw."

"The reserve was advanced in front and deployed to mask the battery which was withdrawn," Averell recalled, "and the regiments retired in succession until the ford was reached and crossed with the loss of a man in the operation." While covering the retreat, Reno had his horse shot out from under him. The mount fell on top of him and Reno suffered a hernia.

As Averell prepared to cross, he remembered the slight Fitz Lee had left for him just a few weeks earlier. In a house near the river, Averell left behind a surgeon with two wounded officers. These men held a bag of coffee and a reply to Lee:

> Dear Fitz:
> Here's your coffee. Here's your visit. How do you like it? How's that horse? Averell.

After crossing the Rappahannock, the tired but proud blue troopers made their way to Morrisville. The next morning, they began their march back to their camps, arriving late in the afternoon.

"The principal result achieved by this expedition has been that our cavalry has been brought to feel their superiority in battle," Averell wrote. "They have learned the value of discipline and the use of their arms." The division commander had more than avenged the fight at Hartwood Church. His troopers had traded blow for blow in a stand-up fight with the Confederate cavalry. "The most substantial result," one Union cavalryman wrote, "was the feeling of confidence" gained during the battle. "This feeling . . . was imparted to the whole of our cavalry."

Forged at Kelly's Ford, this confidence served the Federal cavalry well later that summer on fields around Brandy Station.

A true Confederate war hero, John Pelham earned his nickname "The Gallant Pelham" for gallantry at the battle of Fredericksburg. The entire South mourned his death. Stuart said the loss "has thrown a shadow of gloom over us not soon to pass away." (cm)

A West Point graduate and veteran cavalryman, William Woods Averell handled his division well at Kelly's Ford. His foray there gave his horsemen a vitally needed dose of confidence— something the Federal cavalry lacked after years of being bested by their Confederate counterparts. (loc)

BATTLE
OF
BRANDY STATION
GETTYSBURG CAMPAIGN
JUNE 9, 1863

This hallowed ground witnessed a furious struggle
during the largest cavalry action of the Civil War in the
opening engagement of the Gettysburg Campaign.

This portion of the Brandy Station battlefield is preserved
with the help of a Federal grant from the Land & Water
Conservation Fund, administered by the National Park
Service. Protection of this property was in partnership with
the Virginia Department of Conservation and Recreation, the
Virginia Department of Historic Resources and the Central
Virginia Battlefields Trust.

A sign at Brandy Station, identifying the many
players involved in the battlefield's protection,
speaks to the intensity and longevity of the
preservation struggle. (dd)

The Fight to Preserve Brandy Station

AFTERWORD

BY O. JAMES LIGHTHIZER
President, Civil War Trust

On a spring day in June 1863, the gently rolling hills near Brandy Station, a small railroad stop in northern Virginia, became the stage for the largest cavalry battle ever fought on American soil.

More than 18,000 mounted troopers in blue and gray, their steel swords glinting in the sunlight, galloped across those hills in a bloody series of maneuvers that, by sundown, left about 1,450 men dead, wounded, missing or captured.

Though the battle was inconclusive, it was at Brandy Station that the legendary Confederate cavalry commander Gen. J.E.B. Stuart learned the federal horsemen *could* fight. As the battle raged through the afternoon, only Stuart's leadership and superb generalship saved his force from defeat.

It took a single day, June 9, 1863, for the battle of Brandy Station to transform farmers' fields into historic and hallowed ground. It has taken more than 25 years for the Civil War Trust to save most of that hallowed ground. Almost 2,000 acres have been saved and the quest to acquire more will continue for years to come.

For the Civil War Trust, no preservation battle has persisted as long as Brandy Station, and none have been so turbulent.

The fight to preserve Brandy Station started at the dawn of the modern Civil War battlefield preservation movement. It would take a book to tell the stories of all the clashes since the first hint of a development threat surfaced in 1987.

Ultimately, it became one of the Trust's greatest success stories, with 1,901 acres saved. Of the more than 41,000 battlefield acres saved since 1988, Brandy Station remains at the top of our list for most land saved.

We endured a gut-wrenching defeat in 2007 when a landowner built an anachronistic home at the top of Fleetwood Hill, the most significant part of the battlefield. Atop this land, the day's combat climaxed as thousands of troopers on both sides rode wild-eyed horses in dramatic, mounted charges and countercharges that brought to mind the great European cavalry battles of centuries past.

Ultimately, the Trust triumphed at Fleetwood Hill, acquiring it in 2013. We tore that mansion down in 2014 and are returning the crest to its wartime appearance.

From the very start, and through all the years of struggle, one man above all, Clark "Bud" Hall, has fiercely stood at the breach, fighting every effort to destroy this hallowed place. Hall was joined by an army of thousands of preservationists, from local farmers who fought by his side to countless members of Civil War Round Tables across the nation who wrote letters and sent contributions to support the cause.

The Brandy Station Foundation has been fighting for the battlefield almost from the start. The Central Virginia Battlefields Trust has played a key role, and the federal American Battlefield Protection Program administered by the National Park Service has provided critical funding.

More than anyone, Hall saw the preservation of Brandy Station as a personal crusade. A founder of the modern Civil War battlefield preservation movement, Hall helped lead the largely unsuccessful fight in the mid-1980s to prevent the development of the Chantilly battlefield in Virginia. His primary passion, however, was Brandy Station. Hall, who was a senior manager of the FBI's organized crime unit in Washington, spent weekends roaming the hills and hollows of the battlefield studying vintage maps, reports and letters, teaching himself the complex flow of the conflict.

In June 1987, reacting to the losses at Chantilly, a grassroots group of dedicated Civil War historians, scholars and buffs gathered in Fredericksburg and formed the Association for the Preservation of Civil War Sites (APCWS), which would eventually become part of today's Civil War Trust.

That November, Hall heard the words from a local farmer that would set the stage for the long struggle at Brandy Station: "Bud, I've sold my farm to a fellow from California."

Four months after buying that 500-acre farm, developer Lee Sammis of Irvine, California bought another 500-acre farm on the battlefield. From 1987 to 1990, Sammis amassed more than 5,300 acres of land in 14 separate purchases totaling $21.2 million. His acquisitions covered all of the land on which the morning phase of the battle of Brandy Station took place.

In February 1989, Sammis announced his massive

development plan for the battlefield. He would build Elkwood Downs, a mixed-use development that would be "The Gateway to Culpeper County," featuring residences and shops along with a corporate business park. He promised to set aside a few acres for a battlefield park.

Hall had been sounding the alarm since well before Sammis' announcement. He had accepted the APCWS' invitation to join its board and had the organization's full backing. "Having the APCWS in place enabled us to have some standing right up front," Hall said. The APCWS also put up $1,500 and provided legal help to create a local preservation group, the Brandy Station Foundation, which was incorporated in March 1989. Hall enlisted the help of Washington, D.C., attorney Tersh Boasberg, who had established a track record in preservation battles and would play a critical role in saving Brandy Station.

Sammis began using a tactic we have seen in nearly every preservation fight: hiring so-called historians who question the historic value of his property. Hall countered with deeply researched essays that thoroughly refuted the hired-gun history.

The Culpeper County Planning Commission opposed the first phase of Sammis' massive project; a business complex on 1,475 acres, but the Culpeper County Board of Supervisors endorsed it. They approved a rezoning that Sammis needed in September 1990.

Placed in April 2015, three memorial plaques commemorate the contributions of individuals who played a critical role in the preservation of Fleetwood Hill. (dd)

Bud Hall (left) and Eric Wittenberg (right) speak to a group about the action at Brandy Station. (ew)

"Mr. Sammis won the first engagement," Hall said at the time. "The outcome of the battle is yet to be determined."

The following month, the Brandy Station Foundation sued Sammis and the Culpeper County Board of Supervisors to block the rezoning. The project was delayed as the litigation slowly moved through the courts.

Boasberg met with Sammis in September 1992 and offered to buy key battlefield acreage, but the talks went nowhere. A new battlefield preservation organization, The Civil War Trust, was up and running in Washington by 1992. It began to mediate the controversy and came up with a compromise that would save part of the battlefield, but allow Sammis to develop the rest. Hall and many preservationists vehemently opposed the compromise. The Trust eventually ended the talks and joined in calling for the entire battlefield to be saved.

May 1993 brought bombshell news: Elkwood Downs had filed for bankruptcy under a Chapter 11 reorganization. Sammis blamed the preservationists and their delaying tactics. It had been more than three years since the project was announced and Sammis said he had spent more than $17 million. Still, he vowed to develop the land. "I'm not going to go away," he said.

And he didn't. That August, Sammis announced he was selling 683 acres for $3.4 million to New York businessman James Lazor, who had grand plans to build a $15 million world-class automobile road racing track.

"Mr. Hall, you might not like it," Lazor told Hall at the battlefield, "but we'll build our race track here."

A new battle was joined, and the threat intensified when the county board of supervisors voted 5-2 to approve the project in February 1994.

Boasberg fought back, lobbying against a wetlands permit Lazor needed from the U.S. Army Corps of Engineers before building on wetlands sections of the proposed track.

In July 1994, the APCWS rejoined the struggle in a major way, teaming with the Brandy Station Foundation to offer $5 million for the battlefield. Sammis turned down the offer, as did the bankruptcy court, which accepted Lazor's offer.

By December 1994, Lazor had closed the deal, purchasing 425 acres for $2.1 million. He began clearing some of the land, only needing the federal wetlands permit. Although that process had been slowed by a requirement for a historical review, the Corps appeared willing to issue a permit.

It looked almost certain that the pristine battlefield would be lost. But then Hall and Boasberg learned that Lazor's primary backer was a candidate for governor in New York. They generated local media coverage and hammered away on the preservation issue. Hall approached the man directly with his plea to preserve history, and the financial supporter eventually withdrew his support of the project.

In the spring of 1995, as the Corps prepared to approve a permit with many conditions, Boasberg filed suit against Lazor and his company on behalf of 24 nearby property owners who claimed the track would be a "public nuisance," bringing air, water and noise pollution.

Heavy equipment clears the top of Fleetwood Hill. (ew)

JIM LIGHTHIZER *is president of the Civil War Trust, a national nonprofit organization that has preserved more than 41,000 acres of battlefield land in the United States. For more information about the Trust, visit www.civilwar.org.*

In June, the APCWS made another purchase offer directly to Lazor, but he turned them down flat. By then, however, it was becoming clear that he was in financial distress. Three liens totaling hundreds of thousands of dollars had been filed against him for unpaid bills related to the race track project.

When the Corps of Engineers finally approved a wetlands permit in August 1995, Boasberg filed a suit against the Corps to challenge it. By then, Lazor was out of money.

On September 15, Sammis and Elkwood Downs foreclosed on Lazor, saying he was $1.5 million in arrears in payments. Sammis's only practical option was to sell the land to preservationists. That same month, Dennis Frye, then president of the APCWS, began personally negotiating with the California developer.

"It took a while, of course," said Frye. "We had to negotiate, and it wasn't inexpensive. We had to figure out sources of funding."

The historic acquisition was completed in July 1996. The price tag came to $6.2 million for 1,543 acres. The APCWS launched a massive fundraising drive. The original Civil War Trust kicked in $500,000. An anonymous supporter donated another $500,000. The APCWS membership matched that with $1 million in donations.

But the organization still needed $4.2 million more. The APCWS issued bonds and went into debt,

making monthly payments to reduce the obligation. After the APCWS and the original Civil War Trust merged in late 1999 to become the Civil War Preservation Trust, we paid the debt off with help from federal funds provided through the American Battlefield Protection Program.

The Civil War Trust installed a walking trail and interpretive signs for visitors atop Fleetwood Hill. (dd)

Through it all, the most important part of the battlefield – Fleetwood Hill – remained in private hands. Not only was Fleetwood Hill the site of the climatic clashes in the battle of June 9, 1863, it was the scene of 20 other military actions during the Civil War. As Hall put it, during the Civil War the hill was "without question the most fought over, camped upon and marched over real estate in the entire United States."

In 2007, Fleetwood Hill's owners built a 7,200-square-foot home with two outdoor swimming pools on the crest. Six years later, the Trust had the opportunity to buy 56 acres of the hill, including the crest and the house, for $3.6 million.

Over the years, the Trust has acquired other farms and land on the battlefield to bring the total acres saved to 1,901 as of 2015. We're actively working on a long-term plan that includes replanting trees on Fleetwood Hill to return it to its wartime appearance. We are also establishing interpretive trails and leasing some of the land to local farmers for agricultural purposes.

ARMY OF NORTHERN VIRGINIA
Gen. Robert E. Lee

CAVALRY DIVISION Maj. Gen. J. E. B. Stuart
Jones's Brigade Brig. Gen. William E. "Grumble" Jones
6th Virginia Cavalry • 7th Virginia Cavalry • 11th Virginia Cavalry • 12th Virginia Cavalry
35th Battalion Virginia Cavalry

W.H. F. Lee's Brigade Brig. Gen. William H. F. "Rooney" Lee (w); Col. James
Lucius Davis; Col. John R. Chambliss, Jr.
2nd North Carolina Cavalry • 9th Virginia Cavalry • 10th Virginia Cavalry • 13th Virginia Cavalry

Hampton's Brigade Brig. Gen. Wade Hampton
Cobb 's Legion Cavalry • 1st South Carolina Cavalry • 1st North Carolina Cavalry
Jeff Davis Legion Cavalry • 2nd South Carolina Cavalry (Regt. detached at Stevensburg)

Fitzhugh Lee's Brigade Col. Thomas T. Munford
1st Virginia Cavalry • 2nd Virginia Cavalry • 3rd Virginia Cavalry
4th Virginia Cavalry (Regt. detached at Stevensburg)

Robertson's Brigade Brig. Gen. Beverly H. Robertson
4th North Carolina Cavalry • 5th North Carolina Cavalry

Stuart's Horse Artillery Maj. Robert F. Beckham
Hart's Battery • Breathed's Battery • Chew's Battery • Moorman's Battery • McGregor's Battery

Note: 15th Virginia Cavalry (Rooney Lee's Brigade), Phillips Legion Cavalry
(Hampton's Brigade), and 5th Virginia Cavalry (Fitz Lee's Brigade) detached and
serving picket duty at time of battle and not included in this order of battle

* * *

ARMY OF THE POTOMAC
Maj. Gen. Joseph Hooker

CAVALRY CORPS Brig. Gen Alfred Pleasonton
RIGHT WING Brig. Gen. John Buford
FIRST DIVISION Brig. Gen. John Buford; Col. Thomas C. Devin
First Brigade Col. Benjamin F. Davis (mw); Maj. William S. McClure
8th New York Cavalry • 8th Illinois Cavalry • 3rd Indiana Cavalry • 9th New York Cavalry
(Five companies) • 3rd (West) Virginia Cavalry (two companies)

Second Brigade Col. Thomas C. Devin; Col. Josiah H. Kellogg
6th New York Cavalry • 17th Pennsylvania Cavalry

Reserve Brigade Maj. Charles J. Whiting
1st U.S. Cavalry • 2nd U.S. Cavalry • 5th U.S. Cavalry • 6th U.S. Cavalry
6th Pennsylvania Cavalry • U.S. Horse Artillery • 1st U.S. Artillery, Battery K
2nd U.S. Artillery, Batteries B and L (consolidated) • 4th U.S. Artillery, Battery E

Select Brigade of Infantry (1,500 officers and men) Brig. Gen. Adelbert Ames
86th New York Infantry (III Corps) • 124th New York Infantry (III Corps)
33rd Massachusetts Infantry (XI Corp) • 2nd Massachusetts Infantry (XII Corps)
3rd Wisconsin Infantry (XII Corps)

LEFT WING Brig. Gen. David McM. Gregg
SECOND DIVISION Col. Alfred N. Duffie
First Brigade Col. Luigi P. DiCessnola
1st Massachusetts Cavalry • 6th Ohio Cavalry • 1st Rhode Island Cavalry

Second Brigade Col. John Irvin Gregg
3rd Pennsylvania Cavalry • 4th Pennsylvania Cavalry • 16th Pennsylvania Cavalry
2nd U.S. Artillery, Battery M

THIRD DIVISION Brig. Gen. David McM. Gregg
First Brigade Col. Hugh Judson Kilpatrick
2nd New York Cavalry • 10th New York Cavalry • 1st Maine Cavalry
Orton's Independent Co. D.C. Vols

Second Brigade Col. Sir Percy Wyndham (w); Col. John P. Taylor
1st New Jersey Cavalry • 1st Pennsylvania Cavalry • 1st Maryland Cavalry
New York Light Artillery, 6th Independent Battery • 3rd U.S. Artillery, Battery C
Select Brigade of Infantry (1,500 officers and men) Brig. Gen. David A. Russell
56th Pennsylvania Infantry (I Corps) • 7th Wisconsin Infantry & two companies from 2nd
Wisconsin Infantry (I Corps) • 6th Maine Infantry (VI Corps) • 119th Pennsylvania Infantry
(VI Corps) • 5th New Hampshire Infantry & 81st Pennsylvania Infantry (II Corps)

Suggested Reading

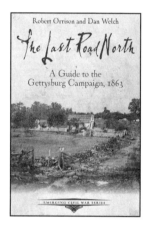

Last Road North: A Guide to the Gettysburg Campaign
Robert Orrison and Dan Welch
Savas Beatie (2016)
ISBN-13: 978-1-61121-243-3

Follow the Army of Northern Virginia's *Last Road North*, with the Army of the Potomac hot on its heels, in this guide to the Gettysburg Campaign. The book, part of the Emerging Civil War Series, offers four tour routes to explore: the Confederate advance, the Union army's route of pursuit, Jeb Stuart's cavalry route, and the route of retreat out of Gettysburg after the battle. Brandy Station was the first engagement of the campaign—don't miss the rest of the road!

Gettysburg
Stephen W. Sears
Houghton Mifflin (2003)
ISBN-13: 978-0395564769

A prolific writer on the Army of the Potomac, Sears provides the Civil War community with a detailed and easy-to-read single volume on Gettysburg. Sears covers the entire campaign, including the battle of Brandy Station and the intense three-day engagement in Pennsylvania.

Seasons of War: The Ordeal of a Confederate Community,
1861-1865
Daniel E. Sutherland
The Free Press (1995)
ISBN-13: 978-0028740430

Professor Sutherland's account of the impact
of war on the people of Culpeper County also
includes a good account of the battle of Brandy
Station.

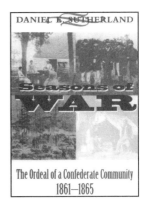

Cavalryman of the Lost Cause: A Biography
of J.E.B. Stuart
Jeffry D. Wert
Simon & Schuster (2008)
ISBN-13: 978-0743278195

At the time of his mortal wounding at Yellow
Tavern in the spring of 1864, J.E.B. Stuart was
one of the premier cavalrymen North or South.
Recognized Civil War historian Jeffry Wert brings
Stuart to life in this full length biography. Wert
examines Stuart's personal life and character, his
military accomplishments and his place among the
great Confederate generals.

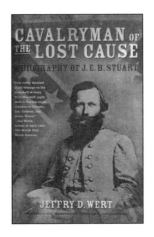

The Battle of Brandy Station: The Civil War's Largest
Cavalry Battle
Eric J. Wittenberg
The History Press (2010)
ISBN-13: 978-1596297821

This fast-paced narrative is written by the
foremost authority on Civil War cavalry
operations. Utilizing hundreds of primary
accounts, Wittenberg introduces the reader to
the antagonists and covers the events leading up
to the engagement, the battle, its aftermath, and
implications. The text is supplemented by maps
from master cartographer Steven Stanley.

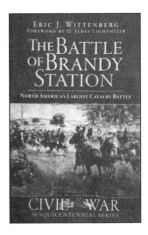

About the Authors

Daniel T. Davis is managing editor of Emerging Civil War and has worked as a historian at both Appomattox Court House National Historic Site and at the Fredericksburg and Spotsylvania National Military Park. He is the co-author of four titles in the Emerging Civil War Series and has co-authored articles for *Hallowed Ground* and *Civil War Times*. He resides in Fredericksburg, Virginia, with his wife Katy and Beagle mix, Bayla.

Eric J. Wittenberg is a leading authority on cavalry operations in the Eastern Theater of the Civil War. A native of southeastern Pennsylvania, he is an alumnus of Dickinson College and the University of Pittsburgh School of Law. He is a partner in the law firm of Cook, Sladoje & Wittenberg Co., L.P.A. He is the author of 18 published books on the Civil War and works frequently with the Civil War Trust on the preservation of battlefields—especially for the Brandy Station battlefield. He and his wife Susan live in Columbus, Ohio.